Recharging
the American Experiment

RECHARGING THE AMERICAN EXPERIMENT

Principled Pluralism for Genuine Civic Community

JAMES W. SKILLEN

The
Center
for Public
Justice

Baker Books

A Division of Baker Book House Co
Grand Rapids, Michigan 49516

Published by Baker Books
a division of Baker Book House Company
PO Box 6287, Grand Rapids, Michigan 49516-6287

Printed in the United States of America

Library of Congress Cataloging-in-Publication Data

Skillen, James W.
    Recharging the American experiment : principled pluralism for genuine civic
community / James W. Skillen.
       p. cm.
    Includes bibliographical references and index.
    ISBN 0-8010-8379-6
    1. United States—Politics and government. 2. Representative government
and representation—United States. 3. Pluralism (Social sciences)—United States.
4. Church and state—United States. I. Title.
    JK271.S547   1994
    320.473—dc20   94-31464

To the memory of John H. Hallowell

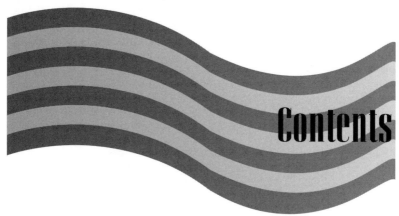

Contents

Preface

The question of whether the United States is facing a serious political and legal crisis falls with increasing frequency from the lips of ordinary citizens. The Center for Public Justice has been at work on this question for nearly two decades, not merely analyzing aspects of the American predicament but looking for ways to reform the institutions of public life. We were greatly encouraged, therefore, when the Lilly Endowment, Inc. extended an exploratory grant to the Center in the fall of 1991 for the purpose of carefully formulating "the question" of whether and in what respects the United States is experiencing a political/legal crisis. This book is one of the products of that effort.

Although written by a single author, the book represents significant teamwork and is now offered as a means to promote further discussion and debate. Our Lilly-funded project unfolded over twelve months, beginning in December 1991. It included three meetings with a core team of consultants: Roy Clouser, Jean Bethke Elshtain, Edward M. Gaffney, Jr., Rockne M. McCarthy, Luis Lugo, Julia Stronks, and Jerry Sweers. Additional guests were also invited in from time to time to participate in the team's deliberations. These guests included Craig Boersema, Clarke E. Cochran, George Herbert Goodrich, Lauren B. Homer, Carey Kinsolving, Bruce MacLaury, Wilson Carey McWilliams, Gustav Niebuhr, William B. Sullivan, Daniel Van Ness, Barbara Dafoe Whitehead, and James Wind.

None of these consultants can be held responsible for what appears on the following pages. Some of them voiced objections to one part of the argument or another. But without those intense and valuable discussions this book would not exist. Then, following the consultations, several consultants, along with additional critics, took a further step and evaluated a second draft of the book. I owe each of them a special debt. Thank you, James Bell, Harold Bratt, Stanley Carlson-Thies, Richard Chewning, Clarke Cochran, David Coolidge, William Edgar, William Gram-Reefer, Sander Griffioen, Luis Lugo, Paul Marshall, Wendy Sereda, Timothy Sherratt, Jerry Sweers, and Bruce Wearne.

It is also my pleasure to be able to say thanks to Allan Fisher, Dan Van't Kerkhoff, and Maria denBoer at Baker Book House who have worked so hard and cooperated so helpfully to produce this volume.

The book is dedicated to the memory of John H. Hallowell who was for many years professor of political science at Duke University and under whom I completed my Ph.D. degree at Duke. Hallowell once directed a Lilly Endowment research program on Christianity and politics. In his well-known book *Main Currents in Modern Political Thought* (New York: Holt, Rinehart and Winston, 1950) Hallowell tried to show how profound was the crisis of Western civilization—a crisis that made possible the emergence of national socialism, fascism, and communism in this century. In our judgment, that crisis has not yet been resolved and the American political system remains very much implicated in it. Underlying Hallowell's thorough and careful analysis of the Western condition was a deep Christian faith that led him to the following conclusion: "Only through a return to faith in God, as God revealed Himself to man in Jesus Christ, can modern man and his society find redemption from the tyranny of evil" (p. 651). Hallowell passed away in August 1991 just as our project on America's legal and political crisis was about to begin.

Our hope is that this book will provoke some fresh and prolonged debates among a wide range of concerned citizens about the future of American law and politics. This does not pretend to be the last word on so vast a subject as America's need for political renewal. It is an introductory word, an invitation to others to consider a different hypothesis, an attempt to initiate serious discussion with others, whether they are sympathetic or unsympathetic with the book's argument.

In placing this book before the public it is an honor for me to be able to acknowledge my debt to the Lilly Endowment, to the hard work of all the consultants and friends named above, to Baker Book House, and to the teaching and scholarship of John Hallowell.

James W. Skillen
Annapolis, Maryland

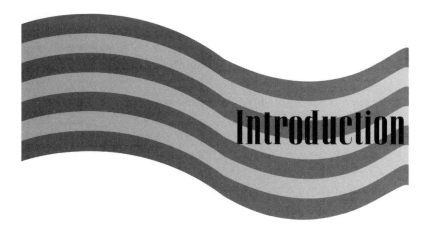

Introduction

America—the great melting pot. Perhaps. But the myth may be larger than life. Slavery, not surmounted without a Civil War, hardly portended nationwide civic harmony; Africans were forced into the American mix on terms different from those that attracted Europeans. Nineteenth-century Protestant reactions to waves of Catholic immigrants reflected something less than melting-pot fraternalism. By the time Nathan Glazer and Daniel Patrick Moynihan wrote *Beyond the Melting Pot* (1963) and Michael Novak wrote *The Rise of the Unmeltable Ethnics* (1972),[1] it was clear that America's multicultural, multireligious mixture would probably never homogenize completely.

Puritans fled to these shores to fashion a new religious community, to become a light to the nations. European trading companies and landed gentry speculated here on an economic cornucopia. Political order gradually emerged as a means to other ends—to righteousness, to prosperity, and then to freedom itself. Probably the most distinctive thing about the new country turned out to be its constitutional design, though no one intended that at the start. Now, however, it is the stability of America's political and legal order that is being called into question.

"America the great"—whatever it was or is—appears to be "America in crisis." Is it possible that the most enduring democracy on earth, having reached the pinnacle of global power, will fail to achieve the full promise of *e pluribus unum* ("out of many, one")? How long can the pot itself endure the heat and fury of its contentious contents?

Our Ambiguous Present

From this point forward the questions multiply rapidly. Does life in the United States actually show signs of moral and cultural crisis, or does a closer look reveal the continuing resilience of the world's most successful and self-renewing democracy? Is our rapidly secularizing society moving closer and closer to the day of final judgment for its many sins, or does this highly religious nation still bear witness to living roots in a spiritual vitality that may yet inspire even greater glory in the future? Have we already started down the road of irreversible economic decline, or is there reason to anticipate growing prosperity over the long term? Is the country really fracturing, or is it merely diversifying in ways that will allow millions more to join in pursuit of the American dream?

Most pointedly, for our purposes here, is the United States facing a truly severe *political* and *legal* crisis? If so, what is its nature? If the word "crisis" is inappropriate, why do more and more politicians, judges, and other leaders express dismay over the country's breakdown or tie-up? The list of complaints is long: growing litigiousness threatens to overwhelm the courts; crime appears to outpace the criminal justice system's ability to catch and correct criminals; urban poverty seems to be impervious to government-designed remedies; more and more families are breaking apart, leaving more and more children in jeopardy; the electoral system no longer seems able to inspire voters or to sustain the morale of elected representatives; the federal government appears unable either to balance its budget or to convince the public of its full legitimacy. Surely these and other signs indicate real or potentially serious dangers.

But perhaps all the talk of crisis is exaggerated. The overall state of America's health may be stronger than its evident illnesses. Our multilayered, multibranch political system has, after all, been highly adaptive throughout its long history. While other systems have come and gone, ours has continued to adjust to the changing temperaments, morals, interests, and divisions of its citizens. Times might be tough, some argue, but give the American people time to make necessary adjustments and the country will continue to keep itself seaworthy for the long voyage into the future. What we are living through is not a fundamental crisis of the ship of state but only temporary confusion within and stormy seas without.

Well, which is it? Do we have a crisis or not? If there are serious difficulties, do they exist at the foundations or only at a more superficial level? If the problems we now encounter arise from deep moral and religious sources, how, in that regard, shall we assess the constructive and destructive tendencies of the American people? Is it fundamentalists or secular humanists who today represent the most dangerous threat to the Republic, or does one of these groups actually hold the promise of national survival and perhaps even of revival? Does the increasingly diverse range of American religions help explain our cultural crisis, or do those many religions serve as a huge reservoir of strength, which we can tap to restore a weakened political and legal order?

The country's present health status appears to be so dense with ambiguity that we do not expect to find quick and easy answers to these queries. Questions about the well-being of a complex society and political order are never simple ones, but they appear even more complicated at this moment in American history.

A Cacophony of Voices

Consider, for example, these diverse, contemporary assessments.

1. George F. Will believes that the Republic is suffering from a serious political illness that requires the strong medicine of "term limits" for elected representatives.[2] "What is in crisis," he says, "is the public's faith in that which most makes America matter: self-government. The acids of cynicism and contempt are corroding confidence in the institutions of collective action and are giving rise to fatalism about events that seem to be spinning out of control."[3]

2. Government is in crisis, writes W. Lance Bennett, because the electoral system has been deformed. That deformation is more complex than George Will imagines, however, and will not be corrected by term limits. Elections have been taken captive by the unreason of media, money, and marketing. According to Bennett, "we have entered a political era in which electoral choices are of little consequence because an electoral system in disarray can generate neither the party unity nor the levels of public agreement necessary to forge a winning and effective political coalition."[4]

3. America is coming apart, warns Arthur M. Schlesinger, Jr., because too many groups of people are emphasizing their cultural and ethnic

diversity above their common identity as Americans. The dangerous dogma of multiculturalism "belittles *unum* and glorifies *pluribus*"[5] in that all-important founding phrase, *e pluribus unum* —"out of many, one."

4. With each camp holding tight to the illusion of its own innocence, writes Shelby Steele, both white and black Americans struggle to gain a moral high ground above the low plain to which each consigns the other—the guilty party. Although racial discrimination against African Americans is not as serious as it was before the modern civil rights movement achieved its successes, racism continues to divide America. "I think the real trouble between the races in America," says Steele, "is that the races are not just races but competing power groups."[6]

5. The "good society" that most of us want is becoming increasingly difficult to build and maintain, according to Robert N. Bellah and his colleagues, because individualistic Americans disregard the importance of "moral ecology."

> "Moral ecology" is only another way of speaking of healthy institutions, yet the culture of individualism makes the very idea of institutions inaccessible to many of us. We Americans tend to think that all we need are energetic individuals and a few impersonal rules to guarantee fairness; anything more is not only superfluous but dangerous—corrupt, oppressive, or both.[7]

6. The weakened moral and institutional condition of American public life today, writes Mary Ann Glendon, is due in large part to the rampant spread of "rights talk"[8] throughout popular culture. Public discourse has increasingly been reduced to arguments over rights, displacing negotiations that could lead to the cooperative allocation of responsibilities. "Legal discourse has not only become the single most important tributary to political discourse, but it has crept into the languages that Americans employ around the kitchen table, in the neighborhood, and in their diverse communities of memory and mutual aid."[9] With the increasing diversification of society, "it has become quite difficult to convincingly articulate common values by reference to a shared history, religion, or cultural tradition."[10] In its absoluteness, says Glendon, our rights talk "promotes unrealistic expectations, heightens social conflict, and inhibits dialogue that might lead toward consensus, accommodation, or at least the discovery of common ground."[11] "Our simplistic rights talk regularly

promotes the short-run over the long-term, sporadic crisis interven-
tion over systemic preventive measures, and particular interests over
the common good. It is just not up to the job of dealing with the
types of problems that presently confront liberal, pluralistic, modern societies."[12]

7. America's problems, according to Alan Wolfe, are not entirely
peculiar to itself. Modern societies generally have more and more come
to rely "on either the market or the state to organize their codes of
moral obligation," creating the paradox that "the less we live in tightly
bound communities organized by strong social ties, the greater is our
need to recognize our dependence on others, even perfect strangers."[13]
"Moral rules seem to evaporate the more they are needed. The paradox of modernity is that the more people depend on one another owing
to an ever-widening circle of obligations, the fewer are the agreed-upon
guidelines for organizing moral rules that can account for those obligations."[14]

8. The crisis of American public life, argues James Davison Hunter,
lies at a level deeper than political apathy, multicultural tensions, individualistic preoccupations, and lack of attention to social institutions
and their moral rules. America is in the middle of a culture war—a
battle of religiously deep proportions over its fundamental *moral
authority*.[15] From Hunter's point of view,

> the nub of political disagreement today on the range of issues debated—
> whether abortion, child care, funding for the arts, affirmative action
> and quotas, gay rights, values in public education, or multicultural-
> ism—can be traced ultimately and finally to the matter of moral author-
> ity. By moral authority I mean the basis by which people determine
> whether something is good or bad, right or wrong, acceptable or unac-
> ceptable, and so on.[16]

What shall we make of this barrage of indictments? Do Americans
today truly face crises on all of these levels? Are they losing their feel
for self-government? Are they divided by a growing multicultural
frenzy; paralyzed by a racial power struggle; blinded by an individualism that reduces public discourse to "rights talk"; threatened by the
degradation of their "moral ecology"; and trapped in culture wars that
might destroy the Republic altogether?

Testing a Hypothesis

The chief aim of this book is to introduce a constructive argument for resolving some of the most contentious disputes about American unity and diversity. We believe that real political and legal crises exist in this country and that if Americans are to address them constructively they need to change both the way they make public moral arguments and the way they conduct civic action. Change must reach beyond attitudes and language; it also requires significant reform of some of our best-known laws and institutions.

In Part I, we seek to clear the ground, sharpen our questions, and introduce the lines of the argument. In Part II, we make the case for a just public-legal order that is built on the recognition of structural and confessional pluralism. It goes something like this: Moral authority sufficient for political community to survive and flourish in the United States does, indeed, stand in jeopardy. Moral and religious-root differences among Americans are real and will not be overcome simply by pleading for citizens to renew their faith in American democracy. In order to strengthen meaningful public discourse American citizens must find better ways to deal justly with the diverse cultures, faiths, and institutions of this society. At the same time, healthy pluralism depends on a citizenry able and willing to engage in public-interest debate and negotiations about the political and legal responsibilities they hold in common. Such debate must transcend "rights talk" and interest-group politics. It demands clarity, from the start, about the precise nature and limits of the political *unum*. The present shape and dynamics of the American political system frustrate these aims of equitable pluralism and civic bonding in several critical ways. Consequently, political unity and social diversity must be reconceived and restructured if citizens are to come to grips with the reality of contemporary American life.

This book's argument is essentially philosophical and constitutional in nature, but, as we seek to demonstrate in Part III, some of the political and legal consequences are quite concrete. In Chapters 8 through 10 we conclude with three illustrations of the kinds of fundamental change that could enable this diverse society to experience greater justice and unity. First, we argue that full and fair legal recognition should be given to various religious institutions, which help constitute public and not merely private society. Second, we recommend that an equitable and pluralistic system of publicly supported schooling should be established so that nongovernment schools, without losing any of their educational independence (and regardless of any self-professed religious identity), are treated on a par with government-run schools. Finally, we suggest that the electoral system be reformed to institute proportional representation for the election of members to the U.S. House of Representatives.

There are many critical issues in dispute today that we do not take up here: abortion; the growing poverty crisis; environmental protection; health care; industrial productivity; the national debt; and many more. Our purpose is not to range so widely but to try to probe to the roots of a "system crisis."

In developing our argument we will carry on an extended conversation—sometimes a critical debate—with the eight authors quoted above, who offer some of the most astute assessments of America's contemporary condition. Their expertise covers the ground from law to journalism, from sociology to history, from politics to religion. Some of what they say helps make our case; some of their arguments represent ideas and convictions we oppose. We could have selected more or different authors. Subsequent to the completion of our first draft, many new books appeared that might easily have engaged us here: for example, John Rawls, *Political Liberalism* (New York: Columbia University Press, 1993); Patricia Smith, ed., *Feminist Jurisprudence* (New York: Oxford University Press, 1993); Os Guinness, *The American Hour: A Time of Reckoning and the Once and Future Role of Faith* (New York: The Free Press, 1993); Robert Hughes, *Culture of Complaint: The Fraying of America* (New York: Oxford University Press, 1993); Stephen L. Carter, *The Culture of Disbelief* (New York: Basic Books, 1993); Stephen Holmes, *The Anatomy of Antiliberalism* (Cambridge: Harvard University Press, 1993); and Douglas Amy, *Real Choices/New Voices: The Case for Proportional Representation Elections in the United States* (New York: Columbia University Press, 1993). The eight authors with whom we have chosen to argue offer more than enough help in pinpointing the issues of greatest concern to us. Here, for example, are several of the central issues around which the discussion will revolve, drawn this time from those eight authors in reverse order.

1. Hunter concludes that even though it might sound "a bit fanciful," the possibility exists for Americans, currently immersed in culture wars, to unite around a new public philosophy that will allow

them at least to agree more fully about how to disagree.[17] Citizens might be able to construct a healthier future if they can establish a context of public discourse that permits them *"to sustain a genuine and peaceable pluralism."*[18]

2. Perhaps, says Wolfe, Americans and other Westerners are beginning to realize that they cannot have economic growth and stable democracies without attending seriously to the health of their families, friendship networks, voluntary organizations, and social movements. If so, then there may be hope of moral recovery in the intimate spheres of "civil society" as well as in the impersonal realms of economic and political life. The relationships in which we live face to face with one another should be valued, says Wolfe, "not because they create havens in an otherwise heartless world, but because it can only be within the intimate realm, surrounded by those we know and for whom we care, that we learn the art of understanding the moral positions of others."[19]

3. Although Glendon is not optimistic that Americans will soon or easily overcome their disdain for politics and recover "reserves of wisdom, virtue, and imagination" that can strengthen them for the hard work of nurturing common citizenship, she has no intention of giving up. She believes that politics can sometimes be the art of the impossible by which we are able to improve both ourselves and the world. Therefore, she makes room for what the ancient biblical prophets called hope.[20]

4. Bellah and his colleagues urge their readers to wake up and, with renewed trust and thankfulness, to forsake the myth of individualism and give attention to the responsibilities of living together in human community. With Glendon and Hunter they see religious inspiration, obligation, and celebration as a creative source for the recovery of political community.[21]

5. Although there are many reasons for African Americans to give in to despair, says Steele, they now have the possibility of freeing themselves from "the tyranny of a wartime collectivism in which they must think of themselves as victims in order to identify with their race. The challenge now is to reclaim ourselves from the exaggerations of our own memory and to go forward as the free American citizens that we are."[22]

6. Schlesinger certainly sounds an apocalyptic note throughout his book about the fracturing of America, but he urges his fellow citizens

to adopt a deeper historical perspective: "I remain optimistic. My impression is that the historic forces driving toward 'one people' have not lost their power. For most Americans this is still what the republic is all about."[23]

7. Bennett says he "can only hope that Americans will convert their anger about a failing government into action."[24] But this hope is strong enough to inspire the conviction that the great day of serious electoral reform—including proportional representation for House elections—may finally have arrived.

8. If the United States is to avoid self-destructing, says Will, its citizens must recover the spirit and practice of self-government—something many now seem more ready to do than they did a decade ago. By establishing term limits for elected office, a restoration of trust between citizens and their representatives may become possible, leading to a recovery of deliberative democracy.[25]

These voices do not speak for us in all or even most respects. In presenting our own case we will explore the adequacy of both their reasons for hope and their arguments for reform. The key question is whether there is a way to strengthen the bonds of political and legal community that can do justice to the legitimate diversity of American society.

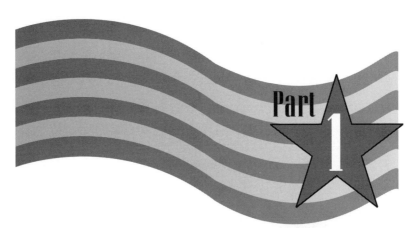

Part 1

Politics, Morality, and Religion

Foundations of Legal and Political Order

The Morality of Law and Politics

Historical experience demonstrates that the shaping of any political order entails more than simply the use of force. Even the most cruel and inhuman systems, which we now denounce as unjust, have been built on moral appeals to familial advantage, divine mandate, historical progress, or the imperative of national survival. Likewise, some of the most violent revolutionary movements have been inspired by moral outrage, whether justified or not, against rulers and institutions judged to be immoral or unjust.

Moral appeal—in the sense of an argument for what *ought* and *ought not* to be recognized as legitimate—is inescapable in the arena of law and government.[1] The popular uprisings that brought down communist systems in Eastern Europe and the former Soviet Union bore witness to the insufficiency of sheer force after the illegitimacy of those systems was conceded. The same can be said for older movements against autocracy in favor of democracy, against minority control in favor of majority rule, against the racist state in favor of nondiscrimination. The argument, writes Shelby Steele, that race should not be a source of advantage or disadvantage for anyone "is fundamentally a *moral* position, one that seeks to breach the corrupt union of race and power with principles of fairness and human equality: if all men are created equal, then racial difference cannot sanction power."[2]

The moral position that Steele affirms is, of course, dependent on assumptions that include both belief in the equality of all human beings and the conviction that state power should be employed to uphold that equality. Political-moral argument, in other words, is grounded in basic presuppositions about what is moral and immoral, just and unjust, good and evil. In the pages that follow, not only will we contend that moral arguments are unavoidable in law and politics; we will also argue that those who make moral arguments ought to become self-conscious about the inescapable presuppositions of the moral principles they affirm.

Levels of Public-Moral Argument

Debates and conflicts over the shaping of law and government entail at least three levels of public-moral argument.

At the most fundamental level, the consequences of debate or conflict typically show up in a constitution that structures the polity as a whole. At this level people argue and even fight for what they believe is *right* and *just* in the basic definition of a political system. They might believe that the highest normative standards for judging what is right are either divine or human in origin. The standards they choose might arise from the deep conviction that human beings are essentially political or from the equally deep conviction that humans are only accidentally political. Many people conceive of these standards as minimal—as a means of mere individual self-protection—while others see them as an expansive guide to the full actualization of human potential through political community. However wide or narrow, however high or low those standards might be, they are the norms to which people appeal when seeking to define the purpose and limits of political/legal order. This is the level at which the political *unum* must be defined in relation to society's *pluribus*, and there are significant differences among people around the world as well as within the United States about what constitutes a just political community.

In our American case, the argument for political unity has most often been a minimalist one. The dominant constitutional aim has been to keep government confined and thereby to protect people and their property from government intrusion. Much, if not most, of the meaning of human life, Americans have thought, is to be found in nonpolitical arenas of experience. In the absence of a common ethnic origin, Americans have done much to develop a political order defined primarily by constitutional rules that limit government. Part of the American "national" identity is pride in government's subservience to its people.

But commitment to a minimal constitutional republic has not, by itself, inhibited the growth of grand ideas and broad moral arguments about the meaning of the American "nation." Arthur Schlesinger, Jr., for example, presents the ideal of American unity as something that transcends "ethnic, religious, and political lines." The American experiment can continue to succeed, he believes, only so long as Americans continue to believe in the goal of national unity above all other differences. "If the republic now turns away from Washington's old goal of 'one people,'" he asks, "what is its future?"[3]

The problem with Schlesinger's argument is that his ideal of "one people" is largely *undifferentiated*; in other words, he does not give sufficient political or legal qualification to the "one people" in order to *differentiate* it from other kinds of institutions and communities in which the same persons bear other kinds of responsibilities. Schlesinger's "one people," who supposedly shape themselves through democratic means, can easily become a people who practice majority politics with few if any limits since, on his terms, they transcend all other lines of distinction. For the sake of national unity, the majority might, therefore, act in ways that easily cross the boundaries of a supposedly minimal state. Such an ideal cannot readily come to grips with society's cultural, religious, and nongovernmental diversity. This appears to be one reason why American public discourse swings back and forth between the extreme poles of individual freedom and national unity, between an unqualified appeal for less government and an undifferentiated call for more government. Theodore Roosevelt's exaggeration should have sounded the alarm: "Either a man is an American and nothing else, or he is not an American at all."[4] What does it mean to be an American and nothing else? A "people" who lack sufficient political qualification (in other words, who do not have a clearly differentiated political/legal identity) can become a political *unum* that overwhelms the societal *pluribus* in a massive way.

At this first level of public-moral argument we believe citizens should be working to clarify the specific character of the *political and legal unity* that integrates a diverse and complex society. Schlesinger's talk of a transcendent ideal of American unity does not take us very far toward that end.

A second level of moral argument concerns the appeals of particular groups and institutions within a polity for legal recognition or validation of their own internal standards of conduct. A religious community such as the Puritans, who were convinced that God had called them into being to serve him according to his precepts, may strive to gain legal recognition—whether exclusive or not—for its moral principles and way of life. Organized labor had to struggle to gain recognition denied it under nineteenth-century laws of property, industry, and commerce. Churches, families, schools, and Native American communities regularly take appeals all the way to the Supreme Court to defend their own integrity. Even those communities (such as the Amish), which think of themselves as entirely separate from the larger political order, typically appeal for the *legal right* to be left alone. This second level of argument is where the accent falls on the identities, rights, and freedoms of the social *pluribus* in relation to the civil *unum*.

A look at American history helps show why the struggle to gain clear legal recognition of society's manifold diversity has been so haphazard and difficult. Mary Ann Glendon explains that two of the strongest intellectual influences in early America—philosopher John Locke and legal scholar William Blackstone—developed moral arguments that grounded legal and political order in the prior, natural rights of individuals. The chief natural right was considered to be private property.[5] In his *Commentaries*, which served as *the* law book in the United States at the time of the Revolution, Blackstone wrote that a property owner "rules over what he owns, not merely as a king, but as a despot. Property rights are absolute, individual, and exclusive."[6]

If all the identities people have and all the things they do must be justified by an appeal to a supposedly natural individual right, particularly an appeal to private property, no wonder Americans have had difficulty developing adequate public-moral arguments for the simultaneous legal recognition of social entities as diverse as labor unions, religious institutions, families, and schools. The unique identity of each of these social "things" is not, in our estimation, reducible to individuals and private property. Thus, American legal and political history has been shaped by arguments that have seldom escaped the dialectical tension between individual rights claims, on the one hand, and majority political dictates on the other. One consequence is what Glendon describes as the contemporary reduction of political and legal discussion to "rights talk."

John Hallowell has argued that Locke took for granted (without being fully conscious of it) a moral order that was broader and deeper than his liberal philosophy could account for. As the inner dynamic of liberal individualism picked up historical momentum, it undermined the consensus about those broader and deeper moral foundations on which individual freedom could alone maintain a secure footing.[7] Consequently, the progress of liberalism gradually depleted the moral capital necessary to maintain a consensus regarding the demands of justice for a complex social order. The Bellah team makes a similar judgment: "The Lockean ideal of the autonomous individual was, in the eighteenth century, embedded in a complex moral ecology that included family and church on the one hand and on the other a vigorous public sphere in which economic initiative, it was hoped, grew together with public spirit."[8]

Unless a political order is clear about the identities and rights of the diverse institutions of society, most of which are not political, then the mere combination of individual-rights protections and a procedurally limited government will not be sufficient to assure justice to a differentiated society.

Finally, at a third level of moral argument, the shaping of a political and legal order inescapably involves judgments by public officials about particular behaviors and public policies. This is the level, for example, at which the distinction between civil and criminal deeds must be made. An act judged to be criminal (murder, theft, and so forth), requires public rules by which designated officials are authorized to use force if necessary to penalize, lock up, expel, or put to death the perpetrator of a particular act. Or, as another example, if a political community such as the United States grants citizenship to people regardless of national origin, race, religion, and gender, then the law of the land will typically disallow particular acts of governmental exclusion or discrimination made on the basis of those distinctions. Our contemporary American struggles over racial nondiscrimination, sexual practices, abortion, the death penalty, and the fair treatment of women and children, for example, reveal the extent to which a public consensus is lacking for arguments at this level. In many cases, arguments about the legitimacy of particular governmental policies depend on the outcomes of prior moral arguments made at the first and second levels discussed above. And this leads us to the next step of our argument.

No Escape from Religion

Moral arguments of the kinds just indicated—about the identity of a polity, about individual and institutional rights, and about the legitimacy of particular laws and policies—also reveal something else that is inescapable, namely, religion. This statement would probably have met with little or no objection up until the end of the eighteenth century and perhaps until the close of the nineteenth century.[9] Today, however, such a statement about the religious roots of moral judgments is highly controversial. A typical Westerner might respond: What have law and politics to do any longer with religion?

Our argument in this regard—to be developed in the following chapters—is twofold.

First, and least controversial, political and legal systems throughout the world have had their historical origins in particular religions. There is simply no way to give a proper account of the emergence of contemporary political institutions and legal principles anywhere in the world apart from a recognition of their origin in Judaism, Christianity, Islam, Buddhism, Confucianism, Taoism, or a host of different nature and culture religions, including those of ancient Greece and Rome as well as those arising from the modern Enlightenment.

Few would dispute the statement that the United States is the product of a Protestant culture—a culture that both helped create and also struggled against various streams of the European Enlightenment. John Locke and William Blackstone advanced that very synthesis of Protestant Christianity and Enlightenment humanism. But owing to its synthetic character, Locke's philosophy of natural rights and individual autonomy was, as Hallowell explains, "based upon an uneasy compromise between two conflicting principles: the idea of the autonomy of individual will and the idea of a higher law."[10] Locke's philosophy of "integral liberalism" was supposed to reconcile that uneasy compromise by its appeal to the moral conscience of the individual. But that reconciliation did not succeed, and its inner tensions help explain our current predicament. At best, says Hallowell, Locke's liberalism

> was an appeal to a Christian ethic that could not survive the repudiation of the Christian religion. For the conscience that was to reconcile the two conflicting principles was essentially the Christian conscience and that conscience could not survive the separation of reason from faith and the repudiation of the authority of the Church. What appeared to be "self-evidently" true to the seventeenth-century mind that was still close to the medieval, Christian tradition was destined to appear increasingly less self-evident as the mind of man "freed" itself progressively from the Christian revelation and the authority of the Church.[11]

Part of the difficulty of assessing the extent of America's political and legal crisis today arises from just this ambiguity of the country's dual origins—in both Christianity and the newer Enlightenment. In many respects the Enlightenment arose as a religiously deep challenge, even an affront, to the basic principles of Christianity. To a certain extent, therefore, the American polity is at odds with itself at its deepest, presuppositional level.

Locke's (and America's) predicament, as Hallowell describes it, leads directly to our second and more controversial claim, namely, that modern, so-called secular approaches to political life are themselves thoroughly *religious* in nature. We mean by this that the deepest presuppositions of so-called secular philosophies function in the same way as do the deepest presuppositions of traditional religions. For example, the argument for a sharp separation of religion from the presumed self-sufficiency of secular affairs (a view that gained dominance in the West after the Enlightenment), is itself the expression of fundamental presuppositions about the true identity of human nature, society, and the world. An outlook on life rooted in these presuppositions is as religiously profound and comprehensive as any outlook ever fostered by one of the historic religions. We may not overlook the deeply religious character of the movements that sprang from the Enlightenment and from various post-Enlightenment movements, including Auguste Comte's "religion of humanity"; Karl Marx's total repudiation of traditional religions based on his new *faith* in a self-sufficient historical dialectic that would eventually produce the "new man"; and John Dewey's "religion of democracy."

Some might prefer to call modern worldviews and ideologies (such as secular humanism, evolutionary naturalism, communism, nationalism, scientism, rationalism, pragmatism, neopaganism, and New Age mysticism) "religious equivalents," or "secular substitutes for religion," or "ersatz religions," or simply "secular philosophies." But regardless of what we call such comprehensive orientations toward life, they serve as the foundation of moral reasoning about good and bad laws and governments. Political and legal reasoning represents a mode of argument that unavoidably begins and ends with fundamental assumptions (preconceptions, presuppositions, precommitments) about the origin and nature of human life in its earthly and cosmic context. No argument about good or bad law can proceed without reference to normative ideas of authority and freedom, of human dignity and responsibility. And all moral reasoning depends on presuppositions held in faith even if that faith is placed ultimately in human reason, or in human autonomy, or in national destiny, or in evolutionary inevitability, or in "absolute" relativity. Political and legal arguments, we contend, necessarily arise from and depend on civic agreements or disagreements grounded ultimately in religious-root principles.[12]

This is not to suggest that every difference among citizens at a religious-root level necessarily entails complete disagreement over every political issue. Nor is it to suggest that fundamental agreement at the religious-root level always leads to agreement on every matter of public policy and law. All citizens in the United States—whether or not each is consistent in the practice of his or her religion, and no matter how synthetic that religion may be—might agree for different reasons that government should be limited, that the environment should not be destroyed, and that children deserve special protection. Moreover, they might even agree about many of the particular limitations on government, about the value of specific environmental laws, and about the legitimacy of laws against child abuse. But at crucial points of political and legal debate, many of the disagreements that do arise among citizens manifest themselves as differences of a presuppositional character, of a religious-root nature. Controversies at the different levels of moral debate over political and legal order show themselves to be extensively dependent on the deepest convictions held by citizens.

Throughout this book, therefore, we will use the word "religion" as well as phrases such as "religiously rooted worldviews" and "religious-root principles" to refer to this depth level of human convictions, presuppositions, and obligatory commitments that give fundamental direction to human actions and moral arguments. Some of these foundational orientations are constituted by self-professed religions such as Christianity, Judaism, and Islam, while others, of a more recent vintage, may deny that they are religious in character. When speaking of a particular religious tradition or of a religiously equivalent community of conviction we will not hesitate, however, to use the word "religion" because we believe that every such tradition and community exhibits such presuppositional characteristics even though in content each may differ radically from the others.

In sum, we are contending that political and legal systems—contemporary as well as ancient—necessarily display religious roots and moral frameworks. The crisis of American politics and law is due, at least in part, to conflicts and incompatibilities at the moral- and religious-root levels of human existence.

Religions as Ways of Life

Two propositions frame the argument of this book.

The first is that religion—in the sense of faith-dependent ways of life or comprehensive, life-directing presuppositions—is inescapable for human beings. The political and legal realm cannot be cordoned off or cut loose from this foundation. To be sure, the political realm is different from ecclesiastical life just as it is from family life, business, science, and a host of other differentiated institutions and responsibilities. But law and politics arise from and are shaped by the deepest presuppositions on which people depend in various communities of faith regardless of whether those faiths are oriented to a transcendent deity. Religious bonds, convictions, and presuppositions about the meaning of life are fundamental and pervasive throughout the highly differentiated social order in which we live. Part of the American crisis in law and politics, we contend, is due to confusion about, and unjust treatment of, the diverse religions that guide people's lives.

Our second proposition is that public-moral discourse in a complex society ought always to be *differentiated* moral discourse. With the phrase "differentiated moral discourse" we mean moral argument appropriate to each of the different kinds of responsibility people have. Since, from our point of view, no community or institution of society may legitimately exercise all authority, every question of moral responsibility ought to be framed with clear reference to the specific institution, person, or relationship that is competent to fulfill that responsibility. An undifferentiated moral argument of the kind, for example, that urges government or "the people" to promote some good cause or to stop some evil should always be called into question, because neither government nor "the people" may be recognized as having unlimited competence (omnicompetence) to address every problem or to promote every good cause.

In order for a *political* or *legal* argument to be clear and adequate, in other words, it ought to address citizens and government officials in ways that do not obfuscate, ignore, or overrule human responsibilities in other spheres of life. Political debate ought to be focused on the normative responsibility of government. Citizens and government officials should not presume that government has authority to rule people in their extracivic capacities as priests, schoolteachers, parents, scientists, business managers, artists, or athletes, as if all human responsibilities could be subsumed under the single authority of an omnicompetent legislative, judicial, or popular will. The ambiguities that often arise from undifferentiated moral debate in the political/legal arena are precisely what confuse, enervate, and cause counterproductive conflict among citizens. Only by clarifying the legitimate public-legal responsibilities and mandates of government can the true weight of civic-moral responsibility be properly debated and borne by citizens. A second part of the American legal and political crisis, from our point of view, arises from a failure to recognize and deal properly with society's differentiated character.

Religions Guide the Interpretation of Society

To say, in connection with our second proposition, that political/legal discourse should have its own, clearly focused character is, of course, to emphasize the limited and differentiated character of law and politics. And this brings us back to the importance of our first proposition about religious-root convictions and ways of life, not all of which yield such an understanding of the political order.

Marxism, for example, has stressed the all-encompassing character of economic production in the shaping of human beings and society. Religion, which Marx thought to be an epiphenomenal or secondary social factor, is therefore dispensable. Other streams of modern humanism place their deepest faith in humanity itself (whether conceived individually or corporately) for which religion (if recognized at all) is supposedly only one among many products of society or the human psyche. For some humanists, human life is conceived of chiefly in psychological terms rather than in economic or political terms. In that case, religion, like law, politics, and economic life, might be reduced to a psychological function or expression. Fundamentally different points of departure with regard to the conception of human nature and society typically lead, therefore, in different directions with regard to conceptualizing political/legal norms and responsibilities. One worldview might, according to its self-interpretation, be completely unreligious, nonreligious, or antireligious because it is organized around the assumption that human life is part of a self-contained, natural evolutionary process unrelated to anything beyond the visible universe before us. But from our point of view such a comprehensive doctrine of reality is as religiously controlling (even though radically different in content) as a Christian or Jewish view of life, which is grounded ultimately in God and the creation order.

Part of the ambiguity of the word "religion" is due to its setting in different worldview contexts. For some people, religion refers exclusively to cultic or pious practices of the kind associated with church life and personal piety. For others, religion is myth and story. For others, religion is a path followed through life in obedience to a god, master, teacher, savior, ideal, or law, depending on the particular religion. If someone were to interpret Hinduism or Judaism as consisting solely of cultic practices that can be clearly separated from the supposedly secular or unreligious aspects of life, he or she would reveal a radical misunderstanding of Hinduism or Judaism. Such a misunderstanding would, however, reveal much about the interpreter's own view of life, which probably locates religion (whether judged to be useful or not) among the multiple functions of human existence. This view of life is no more neutral, universal, self-evident, or free from unproven and unprovable assumptions than is Hinduism or Judaism; rather, it is a comprehensive, life-orienting view of the cosmos that is, on our terms, recognizably religious.

James Hunter is on to something, therefore, when he argues that America's contemporary "culture war emerges over fundamentally different conceptions of moral authority, over different ideas and beliefs about truth, the good, obligation to one another, the nature of community, and so on."[1] Fundamental views of life control not only church affiliation or theological confession but also the understanding of how people ought to live together in public life. Politics, says Hunter, is an expression of culture. "At the heart of culture, though, is religion, or systems of faith. And at the heart of religion are its claims to truth about the world."[2] Thus,

> the distinction between what is "religious" by conventional or technical terms, and what is not, has become very blurred and, finally, rather beside the point. The reason is that public discourse over the various issues of the culture war is almost always framed in rhetoric that is absolute, comprehensive, and ultimate—and, in this case, it is "religious" even when it is not religious in a traditional way, or when those who promote a position are hostile to traditional forms of religious expression.[3]

What Hunter does not illumine very clearly, however, is how these religiously deep differences are related to the confused and misguided moral discourse now dominant in our institutionally differentiated society. Hunter goes directly from the religious roots of culture to what he sees as a bipolar *cultural* antithesis between "orthodox" Americans, who still believe in some transcendent moral authority, and "progressive" Americans, who are more secularized and relativistic. Two things make this approach inadequate. First, the religious-root differences among people are greater in number and more varied than Hunter's bipolarity suggests. Second, part of the reason—perhaps the most important reason—for the apparent moral bipolarity in the "culture war" is the all-or-nothing, winner-take-all demands of our *political* system rather than a simple religious or cultural bipolarity among the American people.

We agree with Hunter that religiously deep views of life are pervasive in culture and politics, but that fact is not sufficient to explain the peculiar character of the apparently bipolar "culture war" in which two sides participate in morally undifferentiated debate about what is good for America. From Hunter's point of view, "moral pluralism" rather than theological or ecclesiastical pluralism is responsible for

America's culture wars today.[4] But to the extent that this is true, it is due in large part to the fact that ecclesiastical pluralism has already been established in public law whereas other kinds of cultural plural- ism have not. In other words, the legal/political disestablishment of the church coupled with equal treatment of different ecclesiastical tra- ditions reflects the *political agreement* to give equal recognition to all citizens despite their *ecclesiastical disagreements.* Ecclesiastical dif- ferences are still great and they continue to diversify, but they do not typically cause political conflict. By contrast, the fact that Americans continue to argue (and fight) politically over many other matters of culture with the conviction that a single, society-wide, winner-take-all agreement must be reached by political/legal means, shows that they are not yet able or willing to distinguish among certain other spheres of society as they have done with church and state. Consequently, moral debate in these instances often takes the form of an all-or-noth- ing, win-or-lose bipolarity, not because Americans are necessarily choosing to sort themselves out into only two religiocultural camps but because they are fighting too many of their cultural battles in a political arena whose rules dictate that mode of combat.

Not until Americans can figure out how to differentiate political/legal consensus, on the one hand, from legally recognized pluralism in schooling, family life, arts, the media, and political representation, on the other, will they be able to achieve a more solid *political* consensus like the one they share in regard to ecclesiastical life. But in order to achieve this kind of pluralism, citizens will have to revise their under- standing of the nature of the political community itself, specifying more clearly the differentiated task of government and the jurisdiction of public law.

We might discover, however, that many Americans, regardless of their ecclesiastical affiliations and other cultural alignments, are unwill- ing to make such a change because of their deep commitment to an undifferentiated ideal of the United States as a nation. If, in other words, the deepest religion for a majority of Americans entails faith in the nation itself, understood as "one people," and if that majority cannot reach a political agreement to disagree about a variety of cul- tural matters as they have about church affiliation, then the ongoing battle for undifferentiated political control of society might continue to intensify in the way that Hunter describes it. If that happens, it will be the consequence of, and a testimony to, the power of a deeply held civil-religious faith in America (shared by people on both sides of every cultural divide) expressing itself through *political and legal* processes that dictate singular, usually majoritarian, winner-take-all outcomes of public contests over matters such as education, sexual practices, the arts, and more.[5]

Religiously Self-Conscious Discourse

This brings us back then to the fundamental importance for law and politics of the religiously deep orientations people have, including those orientations that are tied most deeply to the nation itself. To ignore the differences that emerge in public discourse *because* of those deepest differences is to make a very serious mistake. What is needed in order to engender healthy public debate is for citizens to participate in self-conscious reflection on, and disclosure of, their deepest presuppositions about civic life. Just as an undifferentiated moral argument will fail and cause further confusion in a differentiated society, so too will civic-moral discourse that mistakenly presumes that every citizen shares the same, religiously deep view of politics and the law.

In the United States, to be sure, we have all inherited the same country, find ourselves subject to the same laws, and must conduct our electoral and other civic debates in the same governmental context. But increasingly the diverse human communities and heritages that make up the citizenry of the United States reveal diverging approaches to and attitudes about this *unum*. While not every political or legal difference arises from fundamental religious differences, certainly many do. And it is precisely in order to sort out the nature of those differences that citizens ought to shape their public moral conversation in religiously self-conscious ways. If we do not do this, then differences that are not deep might be blown up into serious antagonisms. Or, on the other hand, differences grounded in deeper divisions might be ignored or suppressed until it is too late to confront them in a responsible fashion.

From our point of view, neither Schlesinger nor the Bellah team succeed in demonstrating this kind of religious self-consciousness. When Schlesinger speaks about *believing in* America's goal of "one people," he does not make a differentiated political argument but rather offers an undifferentiated moral appeal to fellow citizens to keep faith, to hold onto a truth that supposedly transcends religious, ethnic, and political divisions.[6] This is nothing less than a form of religious confession, which cannot, therefore, transcend religion. Schlesinger seeks by his appeal merely to transcend *other* religions and ideologies (such as multiculturalism) by relegating them to a subordinate status. The "religions" that Schlesinger wants to transcend by means of faith in American unity are traditional religions, and he no doubt thinks that his statement in this regard is not itself religious in character. But his argument is a strong, undifferentiated moral appeal to fellow citizens based on what he hopes is a shared faith in national unity above all other differences. This American faith *ought*, in his mind, to entail a common commitment to the nation, uniting citizens at a level deeper than all of their other faiths. Whether or not one agrees with Schlesinger—and our aim is not to deny his right to hold such a faith—one ought, nonetheless, to come to full self-consciousness about the fundamental, comprehensive presuppositions of his argument.

A similar kind of confession, which also appears not to be fully transparent with regard to its religious character, comes through in *The Good Society*. Bellah and his colleagues recognize that the United States (not just American churches and individuals) has it roots in both the biblical and Enlightenment traditions. Today, they explain, newer religions are making their way into the American mix and gaining influence in shaping public consciousness and policy. Need this represent a problem of conflict or tension at the deepest roots of American society, in Bellah's view? No. Why? Because the "American soul" can absorb and transcend all these religious differences. According to the Bellah team,

> We do not underestimate the importance of these developments, but we do not believe that they represent a schism in the American soul, any more than earlier radical religious changes did, as, for example, when the population was altered by large-scale Catholic immigration. These groups, too, enter the overlapping consensus that has characterized American public life from the beginning.[7]

To argue that the "American soul" can exhibit an overlapping consensus, which allows it to avoid schism, is not a simple factual report or empirical description, however. The entire project of *The Good Society* is an urgent appeal to the American people to become a community again in order to avoid the destructive chaos caused by splintering individualism. Apparently there are opposing forces at work at a very deep level of the American soul that could destroy the nation. Schism in some respects already exists and greater fracturing is possible. Bellah and his colleagues are engaged in an undifferentiated moral argument appealing for action to sustain the American experiment as a democratic community. Their argument, no less than Schlesinger's, amounts to an appeal for civil-religious unity—a community of the American soul that can contain all *other* differences including other religious differences.

But what is the ground for believing in the unity of the American soul? *The Good Society* contends, just as Jefferson and Dewey did earlier, for a faith in democracy, faith in the progress of human community through deliberation—a faith that may even be able to lead Americans into a larger global consciousness, a global democratic faith. If, say the authors about themselves,

> we are fortunate enough to have the gift of faith through which we see ourselves as members of the universal community of all being, then we bear a special responsibility to bring whatever insights we have to the common discussion of new problems, not because we have superior wisdom but because we can be, as Vaclav Havel defines his role, ambassadors of trust in a fearful world.[8]

Obviously the Bellah team's argument does not point the way to a form of community that can transcend and absorb all religious differences, because their own standpoint is a religious one, committed as they are to "the universal community of all being." Instead, what the team offers is its own religiously rooted moral argument for a particular kind of community in the hope that it will win the hearts of most Americans and other world citizens. The religious differences in America to which they refer are represented by other religions, which they hope will recognize their marginal status in order to join the larger religious project of sustaining American and world communities without schism. Bellah and his colleagues see other religions as potentially serving a useful function in producing a public, democratic consciousness sufficient to create and sustain human community. Clearly they do not view their own deepest faith as one that could be relegated to the status of mere means to a contrary end promoted by some other religion.

What the authors of *The Good Society* seem to hope is that enough Americans will come to view public life through their lenses to enable a new, communitarian majority to restore the unity of the American soul, which is being threatened by those who live by a contrary faith—an individualist faith that views all or most of life from a self-maximizing, market-dominated point of view. The Bellah team is contending with opponents who stand at the other end of the Enlightenment spectrum—those who are individualists rather than communalists, those who stress markets over democratic deliberation, those who elevate technological progress above the maturation of civic community. *The Good Society* thus attempts nothing less than a rearticulation and reaffirmation of faith in a new democratic world order. It offers an undifferentiated moral argument for the restoration of a public faith sufficiently strong to hold together a multireligious but secularized political community. The Bellah group wants to nurture a "public church" that will put itself at the service of the common good through a politics of "generative interdependence." The glue for such a church and for such a society cannot be just any faith; it needs to be the kind of faith in human community that these authors have spelled out, a faith that can transcend and incorporate all other faiths.[9]

The Particularity of Religious Roots

Our argument to this point not only calls for religious self-consciousness; it also seeks to expose the inadequacy of talking about religion in general terms as a functional abstraction. The political/legal terrain that Americans share in common is not occupied neutrally by any of us, nor do all Americans share faith in general or some kind of religion in general. Rather, we stand in the same political arena wearing different kinds of shoes, using different maps and compasses, heading off in different religious directions. If, therefore, we wish to contribute to a strong, healthy, and common political order, we will have to make a vigorous effort to clarify the nature of our deepest differences. We will need to articulate clearly our different understandings of the norms that we believe should guide the shaping of law and government. Norm clarification will drive us back to our basic presuppositions as well as out ahead into the details of policy making in the differentiated political/legal realm. Such clarification will help all of us both to articulate our deepest understandings of what should constitute a just political order and to seek, through dialogue with other citizens, the means whereby we might try to accept, accommodate, reconcile, or overcome our political differences in order to maximize justice for all.

The argument of this book, we freely admit, springs from Christian faith. This is not to imply that all Christians (along with some Jews and Muslims) will accept the approach we take. Many who take the Bible seriously may have reasons for objecting to elements of our argument. But that is one reason why we wish to put the argument to a public test. Biblically rooted religions share many common assumptions about the nature of reality, recognizing the divine origin of creation, the differentiated spheres of moral responsibility, the fact of human sinfulness, and the heteronomous character of norms such as love, justice, and good stewardship. And yet many Christians, not to mention Jews and Muslims, take very different directions in public life—ranging from complete accommodation to a secularized view of politics to almost total rejection of modern humanism. Some Christians, like many other Americans, may hold a strongly undifferentiated view of the nation while also accepting a strict separationist view of religion. So our approach here is not a positivist one, whereby we survey the opinions of all those who hold some kind of biblical faith and then seek to derive from those opinions an amalgamated, lowest-common-denominator consensus on politics and law. Rather, our aim is to articulate, in hypothesis, a normative framework for a just political and legal order—a framework that we believe is rooted in the biblical way of life, and then to put it to the test in open debate at many levels of public discourse.

Certainly some of the underpinnings of our argument stand at odds with the basic convictions and presuppositions of other religiously deep commitments. If we are correct in this judgment, then it should be evident why we believe in the necessity of public moral discourse that can engage people at the level of their deepest presuppositions while also allowing them to become critically self-conscious about the relation between those religiously deep commitments and the differentiated details of law and politics.

It would appear, for example, that our approach and convictions contrast significantly with those of the Bellah team. We agree that from a biblical point of view ultimate human loyalty should be "to God, in whose hands the nations are as but dust, and not to America. While not infrequently God and country are fused in a conventional piety, it is never forgotten that religious loyalty transcends the nation."[10] Our difficulty here is not with the affirmation that biblical religion requires ultimate loyalty to God. But precisely because of the integral nature and public implications of biblical faith, it is not consistent to go on to talk in general, as the Bellah team does, about "religious communities" and the "role of religion in society" as if all religions share the affirmation just made. Unlike many other groups, the authors write, "religious communities are often concerned not only with the common good of the nation but also with the common good of all human beings and with our ultimate responsibility to a transcendent God. To forget that is to obscure perhaps the most important thing we need to understand about the role of religion in society."[11] The fact is, however, that the religious foundations of all streams of modern humanism are, in important respects, antithetical to biblical religion, as are the commitments of many older and newer religions. Much of the civil-religious nationalism that lives in the United States runs directly counter to biblical faith in the God who rules the nations. From a biblical point of view, all religions (including secularized religions) that reject the biblical God's covenants with creation are false religions.

The extent to which people of incompatible religions can, with some degree of peace, share a political order in common depends, therefore, on what they demand of that political order. An overlapping *political* consensus of some kind may be possible not because of an overlapping religious consensus (such as an American civil religion), but because people of diverse religions agree to keep a pluralistic and constitutionally restricted political order subservient to their deepest and prior commitments—their religious ways of life. But political schism is entirely possible, in America as well as in other countries, if people with incompatible political viewpoints grounded in antithetical religious commitments choose to fight for exclusive control of the body politic.

A biblical worldview, we believe, recognizes not only divine transcendence but also the divine origin and divine governance of an integral, historically differentiating creation order for which the norms of freedom, justice, love, equality, and stewardship (among others) hold human beings accountable to God as well as to one another in many different arenas of moral responsibility. Moreover, we believe that a biblical view of history, divine judgment, mercy, and salvation through Jesus Christ lays the foundation for the conception of a limited state, for the distinction between church and state, and for the protection of religious expression in all areas of life.

A biblical view of life requires differentiated moral discourse appropriate to a historically differentiating creation order. It recognizes the legitimacy of human subjection to moral obligations but it does not thereby defend any kind of human authoritarianism. Christian faith can account for human errors and divisions because it acknowledges sin. But it also points to moral obligations that bind all human beings together because of their common status as creatures made in the image of God. Given the seriousness with which biblical faith takes the Creator and the highly complex creation, it drives its adherents to look beyond undifferentiated cries for "freedom" and "equality" to ask what those cries should mean for people who function simultaneously in states and churches, families and schools, business enterprises and science laboratories.[12]

Our conviction *both* that public life is unavoidably moral and religious *and* that civil government is not omnicompetent emerges from a mode of reasoning that is self-conscious about its religious non-neutrality. But at the same time we insist that making this confession is not to drag religion illegitimately into public discourse. We reject the judgment made by some people that ours is a sectarian perspective. A point of view rooted in the presuppositions of modern rationalism, pragmatism, nationalism, individualism, or socialism has no more legitimate a claim to universal, nonsectarian authority in the political/legal arena than does a biblical view. The legitimate and urgent question is how citizens, who may be guided by fundamentally different views of life, can live together under the same public laws and government. We believe that a biblically grounded approach to law and politics opens up the most thorough, adequate, and truthful approach to this question.

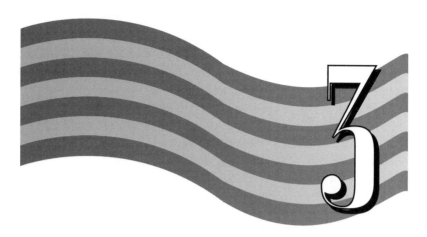

The American Way of Life: An Endangered Species?

Ambiguities in the Crisis Mentality

To determine the character and severity of a crisis in the United States is no easy matter. Undoubtedly, some will object that to focus attention on questions of morality and religion is itself a mistake that needlessly complicates matters. After all, many civic disagreements appear to have nothing to do with deep moral differences and they cut across religious groupings at odd angles and in unusual combinations.

For example, it appears to be true that most Americans—regardless of their deepest differences—still accept the general structure of our constitutional system. Even at those points of greatest moral tension and conflict (over issues of abortion, race, sexual behavior, economic justice, and social welfare) the arguments across lines of political division appear to be disputes about who is properly honoring the system and not about the political system's validity in itself.

47

Moreover, within each area of legal or policy dispute opposing camps typically cut across religious lines. Many Christians are pro-choice on abortion while others are pro-life. Some Christians, Jews, and secularists want equitable public funding for independent schools, while other Christians, Jews, and secularists oppose public funding of anything other than government-run schools. The same can be said about opposing camps on almost any political issue today. Many who consider themselves to be seriously religious stand shoulder to shoulder with those whose deepest convictions are agnostic or atheistic in support of affirmative action, a strong U.S. role in world affairs, or a reduced role for the federal government in the domestic economy. Robert Bellah and his colleagues affirm that there is in America "more of an 'overlapping consensus' among our diverse religious and secular constituencies than doctrinaire theorists realize. Few if any issues in the history of the United States have pitted the churches against the secularists."[1]

However, we must be careful not to identify religion only with churches and other self-defined religious institutions and then to assume that religion is actually confined to those institutions. Religiously rooted convictions and obligations, as we posited earlier, show their influence in every area of life, not merely in church affairs. If stances on political and legal issues often manifest worldview differences that cut across the lines of denominational affiliation, then perhaps the important lines of religious distinction are not denominational or ecclesiastical at all. If we are going to probe to the roots of our political system's relative health and illness, we must not let stand the unexamined assumption that churches actually monopolize religion and that religion functions as an isolatable, outside variable.

In contrast to the Bellah team's judgment about an "overlapping consensus," James Davison Hunter thinks that the situation in the United States has changed significantly in recent decades. For most of our history it might have been correct to see common ground shared by church people and secularists. But, says Hunter, that was because cultural hostilities during most of American history took place "*within the boundaries of a larger biblical culture.*"[2] Today, however, the social arrangements are different. "The divisions of political consequence today are not theological and ecclesiastical in character but the result of differing worldviews."[3] Hunter believes that the chief divide in America today is between those inclined toward "*an external, defin-*

able, and transcendent authority" for life—including public life—in contrast to those who are more relativistic and tend to *"resymbolize historic faiths according to the prevailing assumptions of contemporary life."*[4]

The Bellah team would probably object to Hunter's simple bifurcation of American society into these opposing tendencies. *The Good Society*, by contrast, seeks diligently to show that all religious and secular people should be able to unite around a "new paradigm" of generative care to promote the common good. But the Bellah team draws its own sharp antithesis through American society. The divide is between individualism on the one hand and communalism on the other, between those who wish to reduce society to market-oriented exchanges and those who value human life as something to be fulfilled through mutual care and attention to the common good. The Bellah team may not consider this antithesis to be religiously deep, partly because they identify religion too narrowly with churches. But there can be no doubt about the fundamental contrast of worldviews inherent in their judgment that a new politics of concern for the common good will not come about "unless a new moral paradigm—a paradigm of cultivation—replaces the old, outworn Lockean individualist one."[5]

Whether Hunter or the Bellah team is closer to the truth about the roots of moral conflict in America today, additional ambiguities also reveal themselves when people talk about a crisis in the political/legal system. There is, for example, the problem of a wide range of opinions about the "location" of the crisis (or crises). Those who have their attention focused on a crisis of moral authority do not necessarily overlap with those who think something is wrong with access to our legal system or with a bureaucratic drag on government. Others who see a crisis rooted in race relations may have little in common with those who believe that our greatest political test is over abortion or environmental degradation. Still others who see the conflict in economic terms may have little or no appreciation for those who believe that something is radically wrong with the reduction of political discourse to "rights talk."[6]

Do any or all of these political disputes represent a serious crisis today? Do any of them point to a specifically political or legal problem that can be pinpointed within the larger social, economic, and cultural context of American public life? Do Americans even agree that the political/legal system can be distinguished from institutional and personal spheres of life beyond the state?

Sociologist Alan Wolfe, like Hunter and the Bellah team, is not convinced that there is a specifically political or legal crisis. Rather, he sees the source of many of our public problems in the popular disposition to look chiefly to government and the market for the satisfaction of human needs. This disposition prevents people from paying sufficiently close attention to the multiple institutions of "civil society"—institutions such as families, friendship networks, communities, workplace ties, and so forth. Wolfe confirms Hallowell's judgment that modern liberalism seemed to succeed when citizens were still tied together morally in a diversified society defined by tradition, culture, religion, family, and locality. The problem today, says Wolfe, is that a common moral and religious ethos no longer saturates Western societies.

> As the moral world associated with civil society comes to be taken less and less for granted, liberalism moves in two directions: either toward a reliance on economic models of politics (in which it is assumed that rules of self-interest can bring about appropriate results without civil society playing a role) or into a defense of the state (as the only agent capable of serving as a surrogate for moral ties of civil society that are no longer especially binding).[7]

Wolfe's point drives us back to a prior question. On what basis may we distinguish different realms of moral authority—the political from the market, the family from the ecclesiastical, the educational from the scientific, the profit-making from the philanthropic? An ardent individualist might argue that Wolfe is simply a romantic conservative, longing for an earlier form of society. Most of those older institutions and communities, says the modern liberal, held the individual in bondage. That is precisely what a modern society is supposed to surmount.

Who is correct? Wolfe or the market-oriented individualist? Wolfe or the state-oriented liberal? On what basis can American citizens engage in disputes about what government *ought* and *ought not* to do if they do not share a common moral and religious approach to the normative structure of society? Every appeal to authority—whether to the individual, to "the people," to the majority, to the common good, to "the greatest good for the greatest number," to the American way of life, to natural law, or to civil society, is an appeal framed by one worldview or another, each of which exhibits a religious-root character.

Conducting Public-Moral Discourse

Although this brief consideration of Wolfe, Hunter, and the Bellah group raises additional questions, it also helps illuminate one of the central questions of this book: How should people conduct public-moral debate in a complex, differentiated society in which they obviously hold something in common but also clearly approach that "commons" from a variety of viewpoints?

We might frame the question this way: How may citizens argue with one another in the political arena about what they believe is a proper, moral course of public action, while at the same time recognizing both the contrasting moral/religious standpoints of their fellow citizens and the variety of nongovernmental institutions in which people exercise diverse kinds of moral obligation? Or to ask the question yet another way: How is it possible for someone to argue with moral coherence toward a nonrelativistic conclusion on an important legal or policy matter while at the same time recognizing the legitimacy of both a diversity of moral viewpoints within the civic community and a diversity of social institutions, each of which has its own distinct set of moral obligations?

One approach to this question has been to try to sidestep the apparent moral dilemma by repeating the popular American version of "might makes right." Our political system resolves this problem, some would say, by means of majority rule. Whatever the majority can agree to, no matter how "thin" its consensus might be, provides the answer to the question about what government *ought* to do for all citizens. The minority is protected by having certain individual rights upheld and by being permitted to continue its fight to convince the majority to change its opinion. Majority makes right!

But notice the sleight of hand here. The questions we are posing about America's political/legal crisis concern the manner in which arguments are framed about what government *ought* to do and about what its relation *ought* to be to the rest of society. In our present electoral and legislative systems a majority vote does indeed determine a winning electoral or policy outcome. But those votes come at the end of a process of argument about what *ought* to be the best candidate or the best law. Majority vote is no substitute for public moral discourse at any level.

Moreover, our constitutional system presupposes for its validity a moral frame of reference deeper than majority rule. The reason the Constitution does not grant unbridled authority to the majority is precisely because it recognizes that minorities *ought* to be protected from a majority tyranny. Thus, majority power does not *alone* "make right" but merely makes possible the continuation of a constitutionally limited process of legislation through which citizens are expected to offer their arguments for what is right. Furthermore, the court system provides additional brakes on majoritarianism insofar as it gives authority to judges and juries to deal with individual cases in the light of long-standing custom, common law, and precedent. The power of tradition, in the common law sense of that term, is recognized as having an authority prior to the initiation of legislation, which may then revise it. The court system also permits appeals to constitutional rights guaranteed to individuals and minorities against simple majoritarianism. Our constitutional system affirms certain rights that a citizen *ought* to enjoy regardless of majority opinion. Thus, the larger moral framework that justifies individual rights, constitutional protections, and the validity of common law adjudication is grounded not in majority power but in some other kind of authority. Moral argument in this sense constitutes an appeal to what is *right* or *just* about a political order above and beyond its particular form of government and the will of a majority.

The unavoidable challenge that seems to arise at every level of public discourse, therefore, concerns the grounds on which to base political and legal arguments—arguments for what *ought* to be legislated or adjudicated. The question is whether it is possible to make such arguments without falling into either relativism or authoritarianism. If, on the one hand, one stresses the right that citizens have to hold different moral and religious viewpoints, does that not undermine the universality of the claim of one's own moral argument? On the other hand, if one seeks to act politically and legally on the belief that one's moral argument for a certain public law or judicial decision is correct and universally valid, then does that not open the way to an authoritarian disregard of other moral arguments?

An American Dilemma

Is this perhaps a clear description of our American dilemma today? On the one hand, many insist on the relativity of all moral norms and therefore argue that no one has a right to tell anyone else what to do—and certainly not by means of legislation. On the other hand, most groups involved in public advocacy do engage in moral argument. In fact, they do so with the aim of winning political or legal victories based on their superior moral claims precisely in order to have government enforce common laws on everyone. These groups may, for example, fight for morally correct Supreme Court nominees who will articulate what is "right" even if their judicial conclusion does not reflect majority opinion. And many of the same groups also lobby to win majority power in the legislative arena. Our American dilemma seems to manifest the unresolvable tension between a boundless relativism, on one side, and mutually exclusive, power-seeking moralisms on the other.

This may be what leads Hunter to the conclusion that America stands in danger of disintegrating under the impact of culture wars. Is this also perhaps what characterizes the moral antagonism between the Bellah team and the market-oriented individualists they oppose? And perhaps this accounts for the three-sided conflict that Wolfe describes among market-oriented, state-oriented, and civil-society-oriented moralists. Could it be that an expanding moral and religious diversity in the United States is producing weaker and weaker public-moral arguments as opponents give more and more of their energy to the sheer competition for power? Could it be that the greatest public crisis we face emerges not so much from soundly reasoned moral disagreements over particular public policies but rather, and more profoundly, from an increasingly widespread acceptance of a very low view of politics—politics as a simple power struggle carried forward in the vacuum produced by moral confusion?

Certainly one of the chief fears that many citizens have is that if politics degenerates into a mere struggle for power, then a revitalized religious/moralistic impetus could lead to new religious wars, perhaps even violent ones. If it is true, however, that citizens in this country *do* exhibit an increasing diversity of worldviews, then is it not pointless to hope that those same citizens will be able to find a "neutral" basis on which to sustain a peaceful civil order? If every battle to obtain a legislative majority or to enforce the Supreme Court's minority rulings turns into a power struggle that further antagonizes the losing minority or majority, how stable and strong can a lowest common denominator be?[8]

What Holds the Commons Together?

We believe that the religious-root differences among citizens are of far greater significance in American public life than many imagine, and that those differences have everything to do with the way conflicting moral arguments are framed in a complex, differentiated society. To treat religion—including the deepest presuppositions and worldviews of those who consider themselves to be nonreligious—as irrelevant or relatively unimportant for politics and law is fundamentally to misunderstand human nature and social reality.

Nevertheless, we also believe that it is possible to strengthen the common political order in the United States if citizens will *both* recognize their religious-root differences *and* willingly participate in open political debate of a morally differentiated kind about the nature of the civic "commons," which they share despite their deeper differences. From our vantage point, the possibility of nurturing a common civic effort depends not on the strength of a universal civil religion but rather on three other conditions.

1. First a *common* human and cosmic order *does* bind all creatures. Of course, the nature of this common world is precisely what people disagree about at the root-level of their differing convictions and worldviews. But the fact that humans cannot escape the common bonds of the creation's ecological limits, of the stages of human growth and development, of communication through languages, and of many other features of human society, means that fundamental religious differences are not powerful enough to demolish the common cosmos about which people continue to argue and contend. From a biblical point of view, this is to say that God's creation order, which defines and binds every creature, is deeper and stronger than all human disagreements about and misunderstandings of it.

2. A second ingredient that makes any political order possible is the continuing influence of historical integrating forces—history being one of the creation's inescapable structuring characteristics. Many Americans today may have little awareness of or appreciation for the imposing power that Greek thought, Roman law, and Christian faith had in

shaping the Western legal and political traditions. Most American citizens now reject the religious and moral grounds of Greek slavery, of Roman imperialism, and of the Christian crusades. Many modernists may stand opposed to the idea that human laws ought to conform to divine norms or principles. Some go so far as to believe that human beings no longer deserve special recognition or treatment among the many species of animals in this world. But despite these diversifying and conflicting convictions, the political/legal order that now obtains in the United States does so, in part, because certain ideas, principles, institutions, and habits deriving from a syncretistic, Christianized classical tradition continue to undergird the "commons."[9] Long after citizens have relinquished the moral/religious traditions that produced existing habits and institutions, those citizens continue to benefit from (or suffer under) the politically unifying consequences of those traditions.

Historical disintegrating forces are also at work, to be sure, and some of those forces arise from the inner tensions of incompatible traditions that have been synthesized during the course of our American experiment. In fact, the crisis of Enlightenment humanism and of other faiths today may be part of a movement that is leading the West (and much of the world) closer to splintering chaos and further away from the possibility of a peaceful and enduring public order.[10] But these circumstances do not contradict the evidence that much of the public order in America today is the result of various historical integrating forces.

3. In the third place, and as a consequence of conditions of the creation order and of specific historical influences in that order, the political unity and common legal bonds that presently exist in the United States happen to be restricted to a limited sphere of human existence. In other words, the *unum* over which Americans continue to argue politically and legally is not the limitless unity of the entire cosmos or of human life in its totality. The political order that does exist exists in part because long ago Americans decided to exclude a wide range of human experiences from subjection to public law and governance. We have for some time, in other words, been working at the discipline of agreeing about when and how to disagree. Although the boundaries of the limited political realm may be blurred and much in dispute today, Americans have generally agreed that they do not have to achieve *political* agreement about everything in life. Integral to our

political unity, in other words, has been an acceptance of the independence of vast areas of human life in which different opinions, habits, ecclesiastical practices, customs, and vocations have been allowed to flourish.

George Will stresses this point when he comments that the "crux of the problem in the 1780s and 1790s was that 'the people' were not a single organic unity. The American people had not been of one mind even when pounded together on history's anvil by the hammer blows of Britain's aroused imperial power."[11] The question of what constitutes the "unity" of the American people may be answered only by a response that avoids making totalitarian claims. "Now, the word 'community,'" says Will, "implies unity, but a unity short of unanimity. It is unity compatible with an easy, friendly, neighborly acceptance of differences within a framework of consensus on essentials. But a community needs institutions that reconnect its actual diversity with its need for some unity."[12]

The pressing challenge Americans face today is to answer the question of what constitutes the "essentials" of political unity sufficient to sustain true diversity. What kind of institutions are needed to provide what kind of unity? And what moral and religious foundation can best serve to sustain a political unity that is not omnicompetent?

These questions lead directly to others: Is the growing pluralism of American life a manifestation of an intensifying moral/religious dispute over the legitimacy of the American constitutional order? If so, will it not be impossible to resolve the disagreements simply by reiterating older arguments that gave shape to what is now a fracturing or withering polity? If the foundations of the United States are threatened from the inside, is there any hope of shoring them up or building them, and if so, how can it be done? Perhaps it is time for Americans to develop some new arguments for redesigning the American polity in order to bind themselves together *politically* with renewed moral energy. But if redesign *is* necessary, is there any reason to hope for the success of proposed reforms if Americans are becoming more and more diverse at a fundamental, religious-root level?

What, if anything, do Christians in the United States have to offer at this point that could contribute to political reconciliation and cooperation? If moral discourse is grounded in religious suppositions, is there anything constructive to be said from a biblical viewpoint about the cosmic commons, about our shared human nature, and about the legitimacy and/or illegitimacy of the present political order that might help strengthen civic community? From our point of view, these questions may not be ignored, as if a better way to preserve the United States would be to pretend that religiously rooted moral differences are insignificant and that it will be enough to call for the renewal of "faith in America."

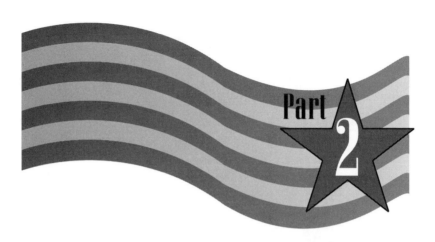

Part 2

Rights, Responsibilities, and Jurisdictions

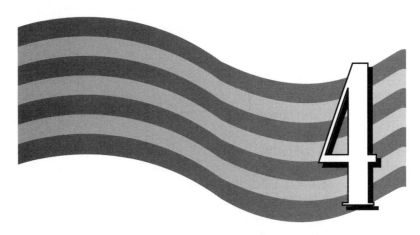

Recognizing the Differentiation of Society

The American tradition of politics and law has developed with considerable internal tension and ambiguity. In fact, arguments about law and politics today radiate the heat of long-simmering and often explosive conflicts.

Liberating the Individual

One current in the broad river of American law and politics has been the advocacy of individual freedom grounded in individual rights. At its most radical, liberalism calls for the liberation of individuals from every authority outside their own autonomy. Freedom is the cry— freedom from ecclesiastical, aristocratic, and monarchical authorities in politics; freedom from too much parental and parochial supervision; freedom from any obligation or contract that a person does not freely accept. Here the ideal is one of individuals throwing off the chains of all past institutional confinements or encumbrances.

Mary Ann Glendon explains that the philosophical underpinnings of modern law typically depict the "natural" human person as a solitary creature.[1] Thus, for John Locke and other creators of the "natural rights" tradition "there was a repudiation of the idea of the human person as 'naturally' situated within and constituted through relationships of care and dependency."[2] Common to the legal systems of all Western countries, says Glendon, "is the idea of the human person as a free, self-determining individual," but in the continental systems of Europe "this idea did not displace older understandings of personhood so completely as in the Anglo-American tradition."[3] The American tradition of rights pays "extraordinary homage to independence and self-sufficiency, based on an image of the rights-bearer as a self-determining, unencumbered, individual, a being connected to others only by choice."[4]

But this aim of liberating the individual from traditional society is possible only in connection with its concomitant aim of political self-government. The liberation of individuals in this framework can be achieved and perpetually guaranteed only by means of a political and legal system that works to advance individual freedom anywhere and everywhere. Without the readiness of government and the courts to respond to the individual's quest for liberation from every other authority, there can be no hope for the achievement of individual autonomy conceived in this way. The flip side of individual autonomy, therefore, is a political/legal system that must, at times, be able to lay claim to omnicompetent power over individuals in society.

Of course, liberalism pictures government and the courts as simply the extension of every individual's freedom and self-governance. Otherwise it would become apparent that the political and legal authorities hold powers that contradict the ideal of individual autonomy. Conceiving of law and politics as the extension of the individual's autonomy has meant, in our system, majority rule in a single-willed political community limited by constitutional protection of individual rights through an independent judiciary. In other words, the supposedly autonomous individual exists in an otherwise undifferentiated society in which law may reach everywhere and rule on anything that those individuals may choose—either by means of their majority voting power or by way of constitutional appeals for individual-rights protection. Thus, both individual freedom and majority rule must, from the outset, be equally boundless in the scope of their jurisdictions. Boundaries and limits may be set only in the course of the ongoing struggle for autonomy and democratic self-government.

To illustrate this point, consider the development of family law in the United States. Marriage and the family, as Glendon explains, were recognized as institutions by common law practices (which antedated legislative and judicial decisions of our state and federal systems) until fairly recently. But increasingly, since the 1960s, the tendency has been to reduce such institutions to their individual members.

> In a perceptive analysis of Supreme Court cases involving the parent-child relationship, Laurence Tribe has observed that, there too, upon close examination, "what at first may appear to be 'family rights' emerge as rights of individuals only." In these and numerous other ways, the law began to treat families primarily as collections of individuals bound loosely together with ties that were increasingly fluid, detachable, and interchangeable.[5]

Our point is that conceiving of the individual as autonomous and the family as reducible to individuals has become possible only because courts and/or legislatures have had the *power* above families and individuals to redefine human relationships and human identity according to the principle of individual autonomy.

The question then arises whether individuals are actually being liberated by this means or are simply being reassigned and subjected to a more universal, all-encompassing, inescapable, and far more powerful "master." One of the reasons why "rights talk" has become increasingly predominant, it seems, is because society's growing complexity makes for less and less clarity at the legislative and judicial levels about how to liberate individuals and keep them free in a highly differentiated but highly interdependent society. One consequence is that many people feel increasingly powerless in a politically organized society in which they supposedly live as autonomous individuals. When they end up feeling trapped and uncomfortably subservient to majority government and the courts, all that may be left for them to do is to fight for their own rights and freedoms over against the majority-dominated society. They become alienated from the common cause of majority rule and become preoccupied with individual independence. All the while, the political system must seek to retain its undifferentiated and limitless claims to competence because there is (in the radical liberal view of things) no jurisdiction outside the realms of individual freedom and political self-government.

"Liberal democracies," says Alan Wolfe, "face discontents because they tend to rely on either individualistic moral codes associated with the market or collective moral codes associated with the state, yet neither set of codes can successfully address all the issues that confront society."[6] At this point in our history, says Glendon, our

> legal and political vocabularies deal handily with rights-bearing individuals, market actors, and the state, but they do not afford us a ready way of bringing into focus smaller groups and systems where the values and practices that sustain our republic are shaped, practiced, transformed, and transmitted from one generation to the next.[7]

Wolfe describes the predicament of liberal, capitalist democracies this way: their citizens appreciate and defend the freedoms they have, but

> they are confused when it comes to recognizing the social obligations that make their freedom possible in the first place. They are, in a word, unclear about the moral codes by which they ought to live. A moral code is a set of rules that define people's obligations to one another. Neither the liberal market nor the democratic state is comfortable with explicit discussions of the obligations such codes ought to impose. Both view social obligation as a by-product of individual action.[8]

If, as we have been urging, it is a vital necessity for Americans to gain a conception of the state's specifically differentiated responsibility, then it is also necessary to gain an increasingly clear conception of that realm's difference from, and relation to, other institutions and organizations such as families, schools, churches, business enterprises, and various voluntary associations. However, if one's predisposition is to think of every such institution as artificial—amounting to nothing more than the consequence of individual action (through contract) or of majority self-rule (through government and constitutional adjudication)—then there is no way to distinguish or qualify the political order's unique realm of responsibility; in principle the political/legal realm remains undifferentiated and omnicompetent—at least omnicompetent in dialectical tension with the originally posited autonomy of the individual.

Limiting Government

This liberal (or "liberationist") tradition has developed in the course of American history in considerable conflict with another stream of thought and influence. The second tradition we might identify with the ideal of "limited government." Here the accent has been not so much on liberating the individual *from* all other authorities but on making it possible for human society to develop free of autocratic, arbitrary, and authoritarian government. In this way of thinking the aim has been to clarify the healthy boundaries of government by means of constitutional restrictions, checks and balances, and popular representation. Outside these boundaries, people are assumed to be responsible not as autonomous individuals but as family members, entrepreneurs, scientists, artists, church members, and more. People should be free from a boundless government so they can take independent initiatives in a wide variety of social realms. Moreover, genuine freedom in this sense means the possibility of exercising many different kinds of responsibility in different types of social relationships without threat of discrimination either from a governmental majority or from an overly intrusive process of individual-rights adjudication.

Within this general stream of thought there is a much greater opportunity to keep asking questions about the differentiation of society: What are the proper limits and tasks of government in contrast to the independent competencies and jurisdictions of families, schools, business enterprises, and churches? What is the unique and limited role of government? What are the limits of individual-rights claims? Within this framework, one will not assume that the will of the majority ought to direct all of society as if it were a simple, undifferentiated melting pot. Here one can recognize the legitimacy of government protecting each citizen's civil rights and developing the commonwealth for the good of all while at the same time acknowledging that many other kinds of social authority exist beyond the boundaries of government. And, perhaps most important, one can recognize that the government's responsibility to promote the common good—whether exercised through legislative action or in the judicial process—ought to take into account, and do justice to, that full range of differentiated institutions and communities.

The Bellah team appeals, in part, to this tradition in calling for the recovery of genuine society. Government, they say, "operates only within the context of institutions."[9] So it is time to step out of the simple dialectic of individual autonomy versus state power.

> We are now torn between our long-standing commitment to "limited government" and the realization that many of our problems require urgent government response; rather than veering from too much government regulation and intervention to too much *de*regulation and then back again, we would do better to rethink the entire institutional context of government in a modern society. The question is not just what should government do but how it can do it in a way that strengthens the initiative and participation of citizens, both as individuals and within their communities and associations, rather than reducing them to the status of clients.[10]

For our purposes we can put the question about the tension between these two traditions this way: Is the American constitutional framework capable of sustaining a strong government that can also recognize the rights and responsibilities of nonpolitical institutions, thereby avoiding the mistake of trying to reduce all conflicts of interest either to those between individuals or to those between individuals and the state? Our brief comparison of two conflicting traditions in American political/legal history thus comes to focus in this question: Is the American crisis in law and politics due, at least in part, to the fact that citizens are laying claim to competing visions of America's constitutional foundations? If so, what role do their religiously deep worldviews play in framing their contrasting ideas of individual freedom, of limited government, and of a differentiated or an undifferentiated public order?

Making Room for Differentiated Moral Discourse

Public-moral discourse today, it appears to us, founders all too frequently on the error of ignoring the plural structure of society—an error arising from the fact that American citizens do not adequately recognize in their legal and political reasoning that human life is constituted by multiple obligations in a complex and differentiated society. In making this argument we are, of course, raising a fundamentally critical question about the adequacy of the liberal worldview, which is oriented by the religiously deep claim that individual freedom is the first principle of human existence and should be maximized. Thus, our questioning is not merely about contrasting legal and policy options that might arise from within the same basic view of social and political life. Rather, our questioning is about *both* those legal and policy options *and* the different root conceptions from which those policy options arise.

We are asking whether there are not significant differences among the views of society and government that Americans hold. Is there not a considerable difference, for example, between the idea that a differentiated society of multiple human moral obligations requires a clearly qualified idea of government responsibility, and, on the other hand, the idea that autonomous individuals are the source of all social authority, including the authority for omnicompetent self-government? Is there not a significant difference between an approach that recognizes diverse types of human responsibility and authority in social life (together with divine authority above all human activity) and an approach that recognizes only individual autonomy as authoritative for everything, including law and government? Is there not a wide gap between, on the one hand, a worldview that recognizes political solidarity without ruling out religious and institutional diversity in society, and, on the other hand, a worldview that considers the nation or society to be a kind of *unum* that can allow little or no *public* room for the expression of institutional or religious diversity because of the fear that political solidarity will crumble?[11]

From the one point of view, differentiated moral discourse is possible; from the other, it is not. From the pluralist point of view, there can be no legitimate omnicompetent community or institution in society, and therefore every question of moral responsibility must be framed in a way that allows for an answer to be directed to a specific, differentiated realm of competence and authority. Undifferentiated moral discourse is misleading because neither the individual nor the majority of individuals, neither state nor church, holds an unlimited competence to exercise indiscriminate responsibility for all of society.

People who approach life without sufficient attention to the plural structure of society typically ask undifferentiated moral questions about what is good or useful for society, and they expect answers that can be given and enforced by the majority or by "the nation" anywhere and everywhere throughout society. They fight many political and legal battles (with the aim of the winner taking all) over issues of sexual expression, educational reform, war and peace, economic justice, art and pornography, or environmental protection. These moralists are convinced that any good that would seem to benefit people ought to become a law. There is often little if any question, in their minds, about the specific, limited responsibility of the political authorities in relation to nongovernmental spheres of life. Undifferentiated problems need to be solved, and society (through political/legal means) ought to *will* with one will (at least a majority will) to resolve any and all of them.

The very possibility of entering into a serious discussion of rights, responsibilities, and jurisdictions depends, from our point of view, on an openness to the consideration of society's differentiated structure. We may find, therefore, that openness or lack of openness to such a consideration is dependent on the quality of the fundamental world-views people hold. A political/legal discussion of family, church, schooling, and other urgent public concerns may require that we probe to the roots of different religious starting points behind the arguments. In the chapters that follow, we intend to sharpen the phrasing of our argument about a pluralist view of society—a normative argument that entails a differentiated conception of rights, responsibilities, and jurisdictions. Our aim is to open a window on a distinctive approach to public-moral discourse that breaks through the undifferentiated moralisms and "rights talk" that dominate political and legal argument in the United States today.

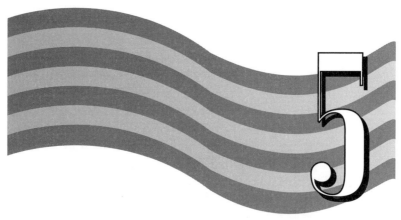

Public-Moral Argument in a Complex Social Order

In order to make an adequate moral argument in support of a just public law it is necessary, we contend, to do more than appeal to majority will or to a general principle of human action such as justice, equality, freedom, fairness, love, or mercy. One must make the case for why government in particular, in contrast to some other authority, *ought* to make and enforce particular laws in fulfillment of its own responsibility to govern the political community justly.

To be fully legitimate, a law passed and enforced by government ought to exhibit the government's competence and jurisdiction. The simple fact that a majority wants a law, or that a law's aim is to advance individual freedom or some social good is not sufficient justification for it. Adequate moral argument for public lawmaking and adjudication must appeal to the responsibility—the legitimate jurisdictional competence—of civil government. To the extent that this is not done, ambiguity and contradiction will arise because a variety of different moral obligations exist simultaneously within a differentiated society. Government ought *not* to pass laws (even if the aim is to promote something good) if such laws do not flow from its rightful competence to uphold public justice. Government ought not to obligate its citizens to do something that violates or contradicts legitimate obligations they hold in their capacities as parents, educators, health-care professionals, ecclesiastical communicants, and so forth.

Alan Wolfe helps make our point here with his critique of the development of modern liberalism. With reference to Mancur Olson, Wolfe says that liberalism began with a minimalist theory of the state and has ended up with a minimalist theory of society. "No longer is a liberal theory of the state linked to a conservative theory of society."[1] What this means is that while the modern state does not want to become involved in moral discussion (it is minimalist, after all), it has nonetheless assumed an increasing amount of responsibility "for raising children, taking care of the elderly, insuring that the disadvantaged are looked after, and establishing the rules by which people's fates are interlinked. Modern welfare states are, more than ever before, engaged in the business of regulating moral obligation, even in the absence of a moral language by which to do so."[2]

We might say that citizens have increasingly come to use only one kind of moral argument (one that is political or legal in character) to reach undifferentiated judgments about every kind of human responsibility. The supposedly minimal state ends up overriding and squeezing out the diverse realms of nongovernmental social responsibility. What Wolfe calls "civil society" (the nongovernmental, nonmarket relationships and institutions of human life) dries up or becomes morally weak (minimal) under the impact of an expanding state—but a state that retains a minimalist moral logic that is inadequate to deal with the diverse moral responsibilities of the people it governs. At issue is not whether government should be a moral actor but rather whether it "has the right to seek the same monopoly over morality that it has assumed over the control of violence."[3]

Wolfe's insight here penetrates deeper than that of the Bellah team. Despite their elaborate discussion of the importance of institutions in American society, the authors of *The Good Society* remain tied to a simple contrast between individualism and the common good, and the "common good" remains largely undifferentiated throughout their discussion. The chief value and meaning of diverse institutions, for

Bellah, is the role they play in helping people transcend individualism and achieve concern for the good of the whole. Politics and government are in crisis now, say the authors, because they are too much beholden to narrow interest groups that do not work for the good of the whole. But what is this "whole"? Who governs it and what are the limits of its jurisdiction? The Bellah team comes back again and again to a largely undifferentiated idea of democratic participation throughout society to make possible "justice in the broadest sense"[4]—the good of the whole. Ultimately, according to the authors, it is through the legal order that the reform of society's institutional structures can take place and that is where "deep intellectual rethinking" is required. In the arena of public lawmaking, where "matters of enduring principle" need to be settled, is where

> Americans can address questions about the institutional structure of the corporation, the proper forms in which public participation in government might occur, the possibilities and limits of other institutions (a redefinition of what marriage and family are, preserving core principles while incorporating new social realities; redefinition of educational, health care, and financial institutions). Such deepening and broadening of the social bases of institutions must, of course, be initiated by the legislature as lawgiver, not just as interest compromiser.[5]

Unfortunately, it is unclear from this kind of argument how the democratically dependent legislature will discern its own jurisdictional limits, distinguish among other institutions that bear social responsibility, and recognize diverse moral norms.[6]

Religious Freedom

Let us develop our argument further by starting with a familiar and generally agreed upon distinction between the jurisdictions of church and state. A law such as the First Amendment's protection of religious freedom, for example, is contradicted, we would say, if the very government that *ought* to respect the independent consciences and confessional communities of its citizens turns around and seeks to *pre*-define religion in a way that violates religious freedom. Most Americans undoubtedly believe that there are right and wrong theological convictions, but for the most part they also believe (correctly, from our point of view) that a good and just *public* law is one that leaves the determination of those convictions in the hands of the communities and institutions that hold and nurture them.

The moral argument leading to this judgment presupposes the distinction between political and ecclesiastical jurisdictions of authority; it recognizes the differentiation of both a public-legal competency and various theological/ecclesiastical competencies. We may not draw from the power of majority will or from a general principle of truthfulness the undifferentiated moral conclusion that government should have jurisdiction over all theological judgments. It is morally insufficient, in other words, to argue (even if a majority of Americans believes it to be true) that since God ought to be honored, Congress should therefore pass whatever laws it wishes about how all citizens should honor God. The missing link in the argument, recognized by most of us, is that every opinion or conviction, even if a majority holds it, is not necessarily something that falls under government's jurisdiction. Government's own responsibility, even with respect to God, must be distinguished and specified both in contrast to and in relation to other institutional responsibilities. This is what we mean by differentiated moral discourse or argument.

Those who believe that human beings ought to honor God should, consequently, take the crucial step of *differentiating* their public moral argument as follows. First, they should argue theologically that out of respect for God's true omnipotence, the government of a political community *should not* even try to exercise omnicompetent authority. That is its first act of humility as a servant of God. In fact government *ought* to acknowledge that it would perpetrate injustice within its jurisdiction if it tried to compel the consciences of its citizens in all respects. Thus, part of the way government should honor God in keeping with its own moral responsibility before God is to uphold public justice for all citizens by protecting their consciences and the jurisdictional independence of ecclesiastical institutions so that all citizens and communities of faith will be able to fulfill their confessional and institutional responsibilities. Second, all moral arguments about honoring God within those nongovernmental realms of responsibility should be conducted without appeal to political/legal power to compel the consciences of others. This is to say that individual believers and church authorities, for example, should not seek governmental power to *force* fellow citizens to heed the theological and ecclesiastical conclusions they reach.

This argument does not give in to moral relativism or indifference with respect to confessional life. It does not suggest that government has nothing to enforce or that government holds no God-ordained responsibility of its own. Our argument is *not* that theological disputes are publicly irrelevant or that they can never be resolved. Rather, precisely because theological questions have the character they do, they ought to be pursued with clear conscience by people and their communities of faith independent of political/legal compulsion or discrimination. With regard to the political order, our moral argument is thus a highly principled one, namely, that for a good government to do justice it must respect both its own God-given limits and the consciences (and diverse confessional communities) of its citizens. Citizenship in the state, for example, should not be predicated on a theological or ecclesiastical entry certificate. Theological truth—including truth about God and human nature that can provide wisdom for public affairs—matters a great deal to a polity. Citizens and governments ought not to act with indifference toward such matters. But the morally responsible way for public authorities to deal with these matters is to act with even-handed vigilance to protect the independent exercise of religious freedom in the common public square.

Our Constitution is not, and ought not to be, neutral in this regard, and government should never act with indifference here. Political authority *ought* to be committed to the protection of the religious life of its citizens. It should never be neutral between religious freedom and religious persecution, between the fair treatment of all religions and the special privileging of one religion. We are, in other words, arguing *as a matter of moral principle* with respect to the jurisdictional competence of the state for the exercise of a particular kind of responsibility that is properly differentiated from the responsibilities of nongovernmental institutions.

Educational Responsibility

Let us take, as another illustration, a more controversial matter—that of educational responsibility—to which we will return in Chapter 9. It is insufficient as a public moral argument to assert that, since it is good for all citizens to benefit from schooling, government should therefore establish schools and require all children to attend them. Even if the general principle of overcoming ignorance is sound, and even if a political majority is ready to do something about it, that specific conclusion is, from our point of view, morally unjustified.

The crucial ingredient that has been bypassed in this argument is the moral responsibility of families and schools. According to both common law and much existing statute law, governments recognize that parents are responsible (competent) to rear and discipline their children. This is as it should be. But family nurture includes a great deal of education, and much of it, in accord with First Amendment freedoms, will be carried out in different ways by an array of culturally and religiously diverse families in the United States. If a majority of citizens concludes that the political order requires a certain amount of education for every citizen so that all may be able to participate fairly in public life, the path that this public-moral argument ought to follow is one that takes into account the independent moral competencies—the distinct institutional responsibilities—of families and schools as well as the responsibilities of the state. Public justice, in other words, cannot be done to children *as citizens* without at the same time also doing justice to children as members of their families and as students in schools.

Government's proper, public-legal responsibility for the whole society may, of course, include the promotion of education for all citizens, but its promotional mandates must do justice to parents and schools by allowing them to fulfill their own responsibilities without unfair discrimination or contradiction. Just as government may require that all churches meet certain fire codes and zoning ordinances, even so it may require that children learn to read, write, count, and master some American history by certain ages. Just as government may require that all citizens pass a driving exam before they enter the highway—no matter what type of car or truck they choose to drive, even so government may require that every child pass a civics exam (or reading exam) by a certain age—no matter where they receive their education. But these expressions of legitimate, public-interest concern on the part of government within its jurisdiction ought in no way to prejudice the moral obligations that belong to parents in homes and to teachers in schools.

These kinds of distinctions, necessary for adequate public-moral argument, are almost entirely missing from the highly undifferentiated discussion of education in *The Good Society*. The authors begin with reference to Aristotle's classical idea that education is a function of the *polis* for the good of the whole community. They go on to show how American schools have been elevated "into something of a secular religion."[7] And then with help from John Dewey and others, they argue for the recovery of the kind of moral and civic education that will help us escape from the present "education industry," which is "simply responsive to market pressures" and which encourages "people to think of their lives in terms of purely individualistic aspirations."[8] Civic education needs to be for the common good, not just for individual, technical, and economic achievement and success. *The Good Society* presumes that a "diversity of education" already exists in the United States, but that it needs to move beyond "priorities set by the economy and the state" to allow

> a variety of forms that would link intellect with character and citizenship. For these to flourish we must make changes throughout our institutional life, particularly in our economic and governmental institutions, changes that would show that we understand education less obsessively in terms of "infrastructure for competition" and more as an invaluable resource in the search for the common good.[9]

The fact is, however, that the present structure of public schooling is under the direct jurisdiction of the state, which, according to the Bellah team, has become preoccupied with economic considerations. Without a discussion of how governments should do justice to the educational responsibilities of families and schools, the moral admonitions of the Bellah team remain undifferentiated and relatively unilluminating. Their argument is a generalized moral appeal for the American people to think more of the common good than of their individual competitions. But who has the responsibility to act to promote the goals for education advocated by the Bellah team? Apparently it is the people in general, acting as citizens through political means, who will need to change the curricular and other patterns of schooling. Bellah and his colleagues leave in its minimalist condition the very society that they fear is withering away, and direct yet another undifferentiated appeal to citizens, urging them to act as a civic body to reform economic and governmental institutions so that government-controlled schools will help government-directed students "search for the common good."

By contrast, we argue that an essential element of government's responsibility for education is the just treatment of families and schools.

Parental responsibility can be fulfilled with moral integrity only if parents are free to rear (and to choose schooling for) their children in a manner that is compatible with their own family nurturing principles. This is especially true when it comes to moral and religious coherence in the training of children. Some parents are, by conscientious conviction, obligated to educate their children in a school run by their church. Others may feel obligated to educate their children in a school whose worldview and curricula are entirely secularized. Others may want a school whose environment is morally disciplined by religious conviction but in a nondenominational setting. Government's public-interest obligations for its citizens should not violate the integrity of these diverse family and confessional convictions.[10]

Our argument here is not morally indifferent or relativistic with regard to either good education or good government. In this case the central principles are: (1) family integrity and parental responsibility for children, (2) academic responsibility of educators in schools, and (3) equitable justice for all citizens under government's jurisdiction. Precisely because government must not be indifferent toward the rearing of children, it must accord the highest protection and encouragement possible to parents whom it *ought* to hold accountable for rearing children. Every encouragement and benefit government provides for its citizens should be provided in ways that are fully compatible with the fulfillment of parental responsibility for children, including the moral and religious nurture that parents provide for them. Thus, we contend that government's responsibility for the education of citizens cannot be met justly if government acts solely on its own authority to devise a uniform (majority consensus) system of government-operated schooling for the direct education of all citizens.

Sexual Lifestyle

Finally, let us take an even more controversial issue—that of sexual lifestyle—to illustrate the character of a morally differentiated argument. The belief that homosexuality is immoral as a sexual practice is not sufficient to produce the conclusion that government should ban homosexuality, even if a majority of citizens wants it banned. Likewise, the belief that homosexuality is morally legitimate is not sufficient to produce the conclusion that government should break down every barrier in society that stands in the way of homosexual practice.

The missing link in both arguments is the intermediate distinction (differentiation) of the public, civil domain, on the one hand, from institutions and communities such as families, churches, schools, and friendships on the other.

A proper, differentiated moral argument, we believe, should unfold as follows: The political/legal arena is one in which government's territorially extensive jurisdiction obligates it to protect every citizen fairly and equitably under its laws. This is not the jurisdiction of parents over children, of church law over ecclesiastical communicants, of teachers and administrators over students, or of marriage partners or friends for one another. Just laws in the political/legal arena should treat all citizens fairly, and this entails doing justice to the spheres of non-governmental life in which those citizens exercise diverse responsibilities. Therefore, just as we argued that government ought not to rule by civil law on theological matters as if it had the jurisdictional competence of a church, and that it ought not to rule by civil law on all curricular affairs of education as if it had the jurisdictional competence of a school, so here we would argue that government ought not to rule on sexual relationships as if it had the jurisdictional competence of partners in a marriage or of friends in a friendship. Rather, government should rule with the authority proper to its jurisdictional competence as a civil government.

Government's competence in sexual matters is a responsibility for the health and well-being of the commonwealth, for life protection and public equity for all citizens. Government ought to treat fairly both those citizens who reject homosexuality as immoral as well as those citizens who accept homosexuality as moral. Those who reject it ought to be free in their friendships, marriages, schools, and communities of faith to prohibit and restrict such immoral behavior just as they are free to exercise similar judgments about other behaviors they consider to be immoral. The political/legal competence of government owes this kind of protection to the friendships, families, schools, and churches of its citizens. But government also owes civic protection and fair treatment to those citizens who believe that the practice of homosexuality is legitimate. In that case, within the bounds of public health, those citizens should also be allowed the civic space for their friendships, schools, and communities of faith.

This argument implies something very definite, however, for those on both sides of the gay-rights debate. The *civil* right to practice one's sexual lifestyle may not mean the *undifferentiated moral* right to seek government sanction for the removal of all barriers to homosexual practice. In other words, just as those who reject homosexual practice should not be allowed to use government to prohibit homosexuality in every bedroom, school, and church, so also, those who accept homosexuality should not be allowed to use government to force homosexual practices into every bedroom, school, and church. The civic-moral requirement that public law should treat all citizens fairly entails, from our point of view, protection of the moral integrity of diverse friendships, families, schools, and churches. People are always, at the same time, both citizens and more than citizens, and they must be free to exercise their multiple moral responsibilities in conscientious ways. In our pluralistic society moral convictions about marriage, friendship, family life, schooling, and ecclesiastical life are diverse and must not be overrun or overruled by a government presuming to be omnicompetent simply because a majority of the citizens under its jurisdiction want something to be done.

In addition to the question of fair treatment for all citizens in this regard, there is the issue of the proper legal identification of diverse realities. Public justice begins with the correct identification of things. How should gay friendships be identified for purposes of legal protection and fair treatment? Our arguments above for the just treatment of families, churches, and schools presuppose that public law can distinguish those institutions from one another and from other institutions and associations. With regard to homosexual relationships, we contend that public law ought to continue to identify them as friendships, not as marriages. Marriage, whether monogamous or polygamous, is correctly associated with a heterosexual relationship. Homosexuality has traditionally been identified as a form of friendship. The fact that a friendship can endure for decades—even, on occasion, in a jointly owned home—is not sufficient reason to confuse it with a marriage. Further, marriage identifies a heterosexual union that might bring forth children and thus create a family—something that a homosexual relationship has no possibility of doing.

None of the arguments offered in recent decades by homosexuals have convinced us that past categories of identification are inadequate or insufficient to permit justice to be done to homosexual relationships. Homosexual friendships can be given proper public recognition and protection without mistakenly attaching the name of marriage to some of them. Homosexual partners can jointly own property. If other institutions, including insurance agencies, want to recognize homosexual relationships as eligible for some of the same benefits granted to marriages and families, they should not be thwarted. If some churches want to perform ceremonies in which homosexual partners promise to remain faithful to one another for life, let them conduct such ceremonies. But for public-legal purposes it would be a mistake, from our point of view, to confuse the words "marriage" and "friendship," or to bring two different kinds of sexual activity under the same word and to grant them identical legal recognition.

To offer this kind of argument about homosexual practice and gay rights exposes, from our point of view, the error and confusion of many public-moral arguments now being made in the United States. Gay and antigay groups typically fight each other in the political arena with undifferentiated, winner-take-all arguments and tactics.[11] Gays feel that if any barrier anywhere in society is allowed to stand against them, it might be used later to close the doors already opened to them. Similarly, antigay groups believe that if any door is opened to gays, then eventually every barrier to homosexual practice will be removed. Gays argue as if government's moral responsibility to enforce equal civil-rights protection should mean that there is only one undifferentiated sphere of moral obligation, namely, the public-civil sphere. Government should act, they seem to believe, as if it has rightful jurisdiction in every family, church, business, and school, treating them all as part of the public, civil-rights terrain. Opponents of homosexuality argue in much the same way but with contrary moral conviction. Civil-legal jurisdiction is, for them, the realm in which various private moral standards (about sex, for example) should be backed up by a uniform (non-pluralist) civil and criminal law so that every family and friendship will take the shape they want them to have.

As we did when arguing about church and schooling, so here we wish to emphasize the nonrelativistic character of our argument. Government ought not to be indifferent to sexual practice. Protection of the health and life of every citizen may entail public-legal restrictions such as the prohibition of marriage between first cousins, blood tests prior to marriage, and laws that restrain divorce, protect the unborn, hold parents and guardians accountable for minor children, and seek to inhibit the spread of venereal and other sexually transmitted diseases. Government's proper civic jurisdiction is one that entails strong and definite moral obligations to protect the life and health and civic rights of all citizens and to guard the public square for healthy access and interaction among all citizens. There can be nothing neutral about this.

But the differentiated character of our moral argument recognizes that civic justice entails the protection of citizens who also inhabit other realms of responsibility in which different kinds of moral obligation must be met by marriage partners, friends, parents, teachers, church officials, and many more. To ignore the differentiated structure of society in making public moral arguments is itself to make an error in public-moral argument—and in this case, one that inevitably leads to injustice. Our insistence on differentiated moral discourse is not, consequently, an argument from moral relativism but rather an argument arising from our principled view of government's responsibility to integrate and hold together a structurally differentiated society.

In this light, consider the following highly ambiguous statement by the Bellah team taken from a context in which they are discussing the great importance of the family to society. "We do not argue," say the authors,

> that the modern nuclear family, which combines the emotional intimacy and sexuality of the parents with the nurture of children, is the only possible or morally respectable form of the family; but because of its importance in bringing children into the world and raising them, it has a kind of centrality and value that we cannot afford to ignore.[12]

If this is a moral argument about what should constitute a proper family, it fails almost entirely. One cannot talk about human sexuality and the procreation and care of children without making a case for what one believes should be a "morally respectable form of the family." If, on the other hand, the Bellah team is actually trying to make a public-legal argument similar to ours for why a *government's* judgment should be restricted with regard to the definition of morally acceptable family and child-rearing practices, then they should go on to clarify the political-moral norms they are using. This, however, they do not do.

Their discussion of family life tries to avoid any moral judgment about what a family ought to be (something that no family can live without) while at the same time trying to advance an undifferentiated moral judgment about how all citizens in a good society should treasure and promote families. "Just as we do not want to romanticize the 'warm' families of the past, of any period when family life was allegedly better, so we do not want to advocate any single form of family life."[13] The internal morality of family life, they seem to be saying, is irrelevant to creating a good society as long as people learn to be more than market-oriented consumers and learn to contribute to the common good. The unique meaning and moral question of the family's identity thus dissolves in the authors' undifferentiated concern for the public good—but a public good that is somehow supposed to entail both a universal regard for the family and a universal agreement not to judge what a good family ought to be.

The major problems that are coming to light in our society, they say, "require the virtue of generativity to solve—indeed, a politics of generativity. The most obvious problem is the perilous neglect of our own children in America: levels of infant mortality, child poverty, and inadequate schooling puts us at or near the bottom in these respects among industrial nations."[14] But who is responsible for "our own children"? What responsibility do those who "generate" children have for them in contrast to the responsibility that government should have for them? *The Good Society* presents a highly undifferentiated argument that does not adequately distinguish governmental and familial realms of responsibility. "Institutional change," in their mode of argument, "comes only as a result of the political process."[15]

James Hunter proceeds in a similar fashion, though he arrives at somewhat different conclusions. Unlike the Bellah group, which thinks that the question of the family's identity need not be settled, Hunter believes that one of the great contests in the culture war is "over *what constitutes the family* in the first place."[16] "If the symbolic significance of the family is that it is a microcosm of the larger society, . . . then the task of defining what the American family *is* becomes integral to the very task of defining America itself."[17] But is it the case, we ask, that a society at the public-legal level must define the family in only one way, once and for all, in order to settle the society's political identity? Is the family really a microcosm of the larger society? Why would it not be possible for citizens to reach a public-moral consensus that government's task is to protect diverse forms of family life and friendships within its borders while at the same time recognizing that the internal moral responsibilities of marriages, families, and friendships belong to the people in those relationships themselves. In this fashion, government would neither treat the internal moral responsibility of the family as irrelevant to the public good nor assume that those internal responsibilities fall under public-legal competence. Hunter is no clearer than the Bellah team in identifying the party (or parties) responsible for making the moral judgments that he believes need to be made about family life.

When Hunter asks whether a republic can "carry on over time without a common agreement as to what constitutes the 'good' or the 'right,'"[18] he asks too undifferentiated a question. If all citizens in such a republic insist on taking every question of "the good and the right" onto the political battlefield, they will, indeed, lock horns in a culture war that will be won or lost in an all-or-nothing fashion. But if citizens can agree on which questions of "the good and the right" belong to the domain of public-moral responsibility and which ones belong—in pluralist fashion—to families, schools, churches, and a variety of other social institutions and relationships, then it might become possible to answer Hunter's question by saying that a just and properly limited republic faces the prospect of enduring for a very long time.

Structural and
Confessional Pluralism

The argument we are developing affirms as a matter of principle two distinct but closely related kinds of pluralism in a politically organized society.

The first of these pluralisms, which we refer to as *structural* pluralism, is the diversity of organizational competencies and social responsibilities. There is a historical dimension to the differentiation of this social diversity, but there is nothing arbitrary about the unique identities of family life, schooling, art, science, politics (and much more). Once differentiated, each of these types of activity displays its own characteristic qualities that cannot be accounted for by reference merely to individual autonomy or to a single collectivity.

The writing of political constitutions in order to mark off the tasks and limits of government arose, at least in part, from the recognition that government has its own distinct responsibilities and is not omnicompetent. Other social structures have their own moral integrity and competence. As society differentiates into an ever more complex array of social structures, government's task of securing justice entails recognition and protection of that "structural pluralism" as part of its legal integration of the whole society. Justice for the commonwealth requires just treatment not only of persons *as citizens* but also of all non-governmental institutions and relationships through which people constitute their lives. A just political order is a complex institutional community characterized, in part, by its establishment of structural pluralism.

The second kind of pluralism crucial to our argument is *confessional* pluralism. By means of the First Amendment to the U.S. Constitution, government is obligated to protect the religious freedom of its citizens. The presumption is that government is not competent to decide on behalf of citizens what their religious obligations and orientations may be. This stricture means that the just treatment of every citizen requires of government the fair and equitable protection of a variety of religions, not because every religion is presumed to be equally correct or true on theological or ecclesiastical grounds but because government's competence to establish public justice coupled with its incompetence to define and enforce religious orthodoxy leads to a *civic-moral* conclusion that there should be fair and equitable confessional pluralism.

Religious ways of life express themselves throughout the structural diversity of society. But the different confessional ways in which people engage in social life do not obliterate that structural diversity. The principle of confessional pluralism must be protected hand in hand with the principle of structural pluralism.

Confounding and Ignoring Pluralisms

Unfortunately, for too many Americans this distinction between structural and confessional pluralism has been confounded at one point and ignored at many others. The confounding occurs when religious freedom is identified only with church life—a social structure that is recognized as separate from the state. In other words, the proper *structural* distinction between two institutions—church and state—is thought to explain and exhaust the meaning of *confessional* pluralism when religion is identified only or primarily with churches. But religion expresses itself through all of society, so confessional pluralism should not be confounded with the protection of churches.

The ignoring occurs when people overlook the actual religious diversity expressed by American citizens outside as well as inside their churches. If people mistakenly think of the public (in contrast to the private) world as an undifferentiated community of "secular" citizens who, by majority rule, may act with one will in every sphere of life except the church, then every law or Supreme Court ruling will be thought of as potentially unbounded throughout the public realm. Religious pluralism, from that point of view, is adequately protected in private life—where churches and confessional religion should supposedly be confined. The public arena is then treated as one big melting pot without any essential structural boundaries or confessional distinctions. Not only is the religious (or worldview) diversity of citizens thereby ignored in public, but so too, at times, is the structural pluralism of schools, family life, and different kinds of corporations.

What is needed we believe, is a much clearer recognition of distinct rights, responsibilities, and jurisdictions in society so citizens and government will no longer be able to confound or ignore structural and confessional pluralisms. Mary Ann Glendon and Raul F. Yanes help point up this need. A proper reading of the First Amendment, they write, "suggests that individual free exercise cannot be treated in isolation from the need of religious associations and their members for a protected sphere within which they can provide for the definition, development, and transmission of their own beliefs and practices."[1] The problem in contemporary American jurisprudence is that the interpretation of the First Amendment is typically "geared only to the individual, the state, and the market" and thus is unable "to take account of the social dimensions of human personhood, and of the social environments that individual human beings require in order to fully develop their potential."[2]

In early America, diverse church bodies existed, and a few of them enjoyed an established status first in the colonies and then in some of the states. The federal Constitution's First Amendment did not try immediately to disestablish state churches but sought only to guarantee that the federal government would not establish a church or give preferential treatment to one religion. However, in effect, the First Amendment also laid the basis for the later disestablishment of state churches. The structural distinction between church and state thus came to be recognized constitutionally as part of the Republic's limits—as one expression of its lack of omnicompetence.

But the First Amendment dealt with more than the nonestablishment or disestablishment of churches. The *structural* distinction between church and state is not all that was constitutionalized. Persons, not merely churches, are recognized as having *religious freedom*. Citizens should be free to follow their conscience in obedience to God. If government, therefore, is not competent to define and enforce a single true religion, and if, at the same time, it is supposed to do justice to all of its citizens, then religious freedom implies two distinct though interrelated things. The first is that religiously free citizens must be treated fairly and equitably in their practice of *different* religions (confessional pluralism) in all areas of life. And in the second place, if one of the ways they choose to practice their religions is through organized churches, then a *diversity* of churches—structurally distinct from the state—must be recognized and treated with equal protection (structural pluralism).

Notice here the important point about *diverse* religious practices among free citizens. The Constitution does not give government the right to confound religion with, or to confine religion to, institutional churches. Insofar as religions express themselves in organized institutions of worship, confession, theology, and discipline, then naturally a diverse array of churches will appear, each deserving equal treatment under the law. But the often overlooked fact is that religions also express themselves outside the walls of churches. Believers of different stripes may be obligated by their faith to rear their children in specific ways, to eat different kinds of food, to pursue their occupations in a certain manner, and to exercise their responsibilities distinctively in a variety of professions such as medicine, law, and even politics itself. For government to confound confessional and structural pluralism is to restrict religious freedom to church life and private conscience—a restriction that actually violates the religions of many people.

That type of confounding can also foster the illegitimate practice of *ignoring* the distinction between structural and confessional pluralism. If religion is mistakenly thought to be confined to churches, and if a public melting-pot ideal hides from view the reality of societal differentiation, then it is entirely possible that governments might take over responsibility for education (for example) in a way that overlooks and violates *both* the structurally distinct character of families and schools *as well as* the religious diversity that citizens might wish to express in education. If, however, citizens are given legitimate protection under the Constitution to practice their religions freely (confessional pluralism), then all citizens should be free to conduct family life, schooling, and other social practices (structural pluralism) in ways that are consistent with the obligations of their deepest presuppositions and faiths.

Must Pluralism Lead to Culture Wars?

Most of the authors with whom we have been arguing in these pages do not exhibit sufficiently differentiated modes of moral discourse because they have not adequately confronted the implications of structural and confessional pluralism. Let us return to James Hunter's *Culture Wars* to illustrate the point.

Early in his book, Hunter defines "cultural conflict very simply as political and social hostility rooted in different systems of moral understanding. The end to which these hostilities tend is the domination of one cultural and moral ethos over all others."[3] The implication of this statement is that in circumstances of hostility a "cultural and moral ethos" is something that seeks "domination" throughout the political and social order. A moral ethos might not be articulated in a conscious worldview, says Hunter, but it may express itself as a polarizing impulse or tendency in culture.[4] Most Americans might not even take sides between or among these competing "impulses" or "tendencies," he says, further qualifying his judgment about the nature of cultural conflict. But the "polarizing tendency" shows up nonetheless and most sharply "in the organizations and spokespeople who have an interest in promoting a particular position on a social issue."[5]

Notice how Hunter moves from a statement about undifferentiated moral/cultural conflict (which arises, he argues elsewhere, from religious depths), through a series of moral/psychological qualifications, to a conclusion about organized interest competition. In the process, however, he pays too little attention to society's *structurally* differentiated character. If we follow him closely, we must ask how, if the cultural conflict is so all-pervasive and deep, can most people avoid embracing a moral position uncritically and even remain in "a vast middle ground between the polarizing impulses"?[6] Why, if most people really stand in a middle position, do they allow themselves to get carried along by organizations and spokespeople who promote positions on particular social issues in a highly polarizing way?

We can account for Hunter's position here by turning a light on the structural and confessional diversity of American society. Hunter notes that one of the early American "culture wars" was between the Protestant majority and the newly immigrating Catholic minority, beginning early in the nineteenth century. Their cultural struggle came to a head over schooling when Protestants used political means to secure public privilege for their schools, legally discriminating against Catholic schools.[7] By the middle of the twentieth century, however, the older struggle between Catholics and Protestants had faded away because "the changing structure of American pluralism made the old antagonism obsolete."[8] Today the basic cultural conflict is between a more secular progressivism, on the one hand, and a more religious orthodoxy, on the other—both of which cut through Protestant and Catholic communities.

What Hunter's assessment fails to illuminate, however, is that while the confessionally grounded Protestant/Catholic struggles of the nineteenth century took place on a number of fronts, Catholics ended up with roughly the same public-legal recognition that Protestants enjoyed in their churches, families, and (for the most part) employment. But Catholics lost the political battle over education, where a majority victory allowed those who were mostly Protestant to establish their schools as public schools while forcing Catholic schools into a private status. Yet even in that sphere, Catholic schools were not banned altogether. Consider the difference here between the position of Catholics and that of black slaves, for example, or even the difference between the Catholic/Protestant conflicts over schooling and the conflicts between Northern and Southern cultures and economies that led to the Civil War.

Our point is that Catholics and Protestants did not stand in as much of a religio/moral/cultural opposition to one another in the mid-nineteenth century as Hunter's assessment implies. Their conflict might have taken the country into a civil war if, for example, the Protestant majority had decided to try to outlaw Catholic schools or to close down Catholic churches altogether. Catholics and Protestants did not, in other words, take all of their moral and theological differences onto the political battlefield. Their "war" was chiefly a political conflict over the status of schools, and, unfortunately and unnecessarily, it was decided by a winner-take-all contest. Today, disagreements between Catholics and Protestants are not obsolete but are, for the most part, dealt with outside the arena of political combat.

The fact that, as Hunter says, the school wars today are between different antagonists says more, we believe, about the nature of the *political* structure of education than it does about the shifting moral and religious commitments of American citizens. Today there are far more religious and moral differences in the United States than existed in the nineteenth century, so "cultural conflict" at the root level is more diverse than Hunter's bipolarization scheme allows. On the other hand, if we couple the fact that the political system continues to be defined largely by simple majoritarian processes (in which citizens must contend for winner-take-all stakes) with the fact that this political system still discriminates severely against nongovernment schools (regardless of their religious commitments), we will see that the contemporary conflict over schooling represents not an undifferentiated, bipolar culture war but a specifically *political* conflict over the manner in which justice should be done to the confessional and educational diversity of the American people.

The conflicts that Hunter is trying to explain require a somewhat different mode of analysis, in our opinion. The focus of attention should be directed to the specific *structure* of the political system in its relation to other social institutions and relationships. And a critical inquiry into the roots of *confessional pluralism* should seek, in particular, to illuminate the origin of contrasting conceptions of that political order. Trying to identify two (largely undifferentiated) sides of a "cultural war" by tracking the lineups in particular *political* battles does not take us very far. What Hunter sees as today's dominant conflict between a culturally "orthodox" tendency and a culturally "progressive" tendency is too artificial and elusive. Some political conflicts may give the appearance of such a polarization, but they do not adequately represent the real cultural and religious lines of conflict. Moreover, his approach does little to show what a *just* outcome of those battles ought to be, or what is morally normative on either the "orthodox" or the "progressive" side.

Consequently, when Hunter comes to the end of his book and tries to argue that both sides need to develop a public philosophy that will allow them to live with their deepest differences, his challenge packs little moral punch. If he is implying that a deeper moral ground of agreement may already exist to support both sides, this flies in the face of the book's entire argument. If, on the other hand, he is trying to suggest a new, *politically pluralistic* solution, he comes up short because nothing in his book prepares the reader for a differentiated political-moral argument sufficient to bear the weight of his demand.[9]

Most of the battles that Hunter describes exhibit typical bipolar dynamics because the present structure of the state (the legal and governmental order) does not do sufficient justice to the confessional and structural diversity of American society. At a religiocultural level, therefore, our chief question must be directed to the source of that dominant idea of the American political order and its systems of representation rather than to lose alliances and oppositions that may form within it. And an adequate moral argument for dealing justly with confessional and social differences must take the form of a normative political argument. Only by following such a course will it be possible to explain the significance of religious-root differences in a society that is as structurally and confessionally differentiated as is ours.

Societal Pluralism and Political Unity

The outcome of our *moral argument*, which contends both for uncoerced religion and for the recognition of societal differentiation, is an outcome that in no way conflicts with the norm of *integrative* public justice for a single political community. It simply extends with consistency two principles already enshrined in the Constitution. It seeks, first, to safeguard religious freedom in all of life, not allowing government to confine religion illegitimately within the institutional limits of church life, and, second, to safeguard the legitimate spheres of responsibility outside government's jurisdiction. By insisting on these two elements of pluralism, our argument aims to secure and to strengthen fundamental pillars of a unifying and integrative civil order. Only laws that treat all citizens fairly in their actual social and cultural diversity (the *pluribus*) will be able to carry the moral force necessary to bind people together legally as citizens in a single republic (the *unum*).

This argument has important implications not only for churches, families, friendships, and schooling, but also for political participation itself, as we will argue in more detail in Chapter 10. Just as we object to the confounding of education and government, arguing (on both confessional and structural pluralist grounds) for the differentiation of their jurisdictions, so too we wish to argue for a clearer differentiation of *governmental* institutions from those voluntary *electoral* organizations through which citizens work to gain representation. It is true, to be sure, that our state and federal governments do not now own or control the political parties (or vice versa) as happens in totalitarian systems. At the same time, however, our election laws and the dominant political culture do encourage citizens mistakenly to confound the electoral and governing processes. The purpose of both elections and lawmaking is thought to be the same: to obtain a majority consensus that can express the single will of the people exercising self-government.

But what if, as in church life and education, people hold different views of what government ought to be and to do? What if an increasing number of citizens hold political views that belong only to a minority of the population? What if our country is moving toward the point where no single party coalition—even the largest one—any longer represents a genuine majority? Our present electoral system says to citizens, in effect, that they have no choice but to try to organize majority coalitions for electoral purposes even if the consensus achieved by those coalitions is relatively artificial and superficial. If citizens do not want to play the game by these rules, then they must learn to be happy trying to express their views outside Congress and the state legislatures as unelectable minorities. If those unelectable minorities want to gain representation at election time, either they have to voice views different from the ones they hold most deeply, thus compromising themselves, or they have to be willing to accommodate themselves, for electoral purposes, to a lowest common denominator sufficient to produce a 51 percent majority, which is then allowed to "take all."

From our standpoint, however, an important and more complete structural distinction between electoral representation and government ought to be recognized. *Government* must, indeed, have at its disposal the means of bringing legislative debate to conclusion in order to produce laws. On matters over which governments have the responsibility to deliberate and rule, decisions must finally be reached—whether by simple majority, two-thirds majority, or three-fourths majority vote. In our federal government, a bill cannot become law without this kind of deliberation and voting by both Senate and House on identical bills followed by the president's signature. To this process we offer no objection.

The purpose of *electoral representation*, however, is very different from that of governing. Unlike the governing process, there is no need for the electoral process to reach a winner-take-all conclusion. The purpose of elections is to begin public debate, not to end it by giving 51 percent of the voters total victory. The purpose of representation is not to reach a premature majority conclusion but to allow the people to be represented in legislative bodies so their representatives can continue with serious deliberation toward legislative ends. In order for the people to be adequately represented in legislatures and Congress, therefore, an electoral system is needed that comes as close as possible to making every vote count. The actual diversity of viewpoints— of public moral arguments about the task of government—needs to be represented in legislative deliberation. If this were to be achieved in American politics, it would radically change the often superficial polarization that occurs in the extralegislative, all-or-nothing, interest-group competition that Hunter interprets as evidence of a general bipolar, cultural divide among the American people.

Our argument here about electoral representation is not intended to encourage either relativism or chaos. It is an argument for a more solid basis of political unity similar to our argument for a new *political* agreement about religious, educational, and sexual pluralism. In essence, we are proposing the displacement of one conception of representation by another, just as Americans, early in their history, displaced one conception of the state (one requiring an ecclesiastical establishment) with another conception of the state (one requiring an ecclesiastical disestablishment). The political order was not fractured by that move; to the contrary, ecclesiastical disestablishment helped *unify* the new Republic as a politically qualified entity.

In a similar fashion, we are suggesting that the present single-willed majoritarian conception of the body politic be replaced by a pluralist conception of the single body politic. Melting-pot majoritarians, who have always believed that the state can survive only on the basis of a uniform political culture (conveyed to children in government-run schools and expressed through winner-take-all majority voting), may be unhappy with such a displacement. In fact, if their political vision arises from a religiously deep commitment to the ideal of an undifferentiated American nation, some of them will fight hard to hold onto the present system rather than give in to reforms of the kind we are suggesting. Under the terms of our proposal, the vision of a uniform culture sustained by simple majority control of government would no longer be able to dominate the public world. That vision or ideology would have political power only proportionate to the number of its adherents.

To displace that lowest-common-denominator majoritarian ideal we need a richer and more realistic conception of America's diversity in order to make it possible for all citizens to express themselves in authentic debate about how they want to be bound together politically. If electoral minorities as well as electoral majorities were able to be represented according to their convictions in state and federal legislatures, we would all have the opportunity to reach a better understanding of the different views of political life held by American citizens and would be able to see the proportion of the entire body politic that holds each view. Legislative deliberation would then proceed after a variety of parties has obtained fair representation. Members of Congress, adequately representing the American people in their true diversity, would then work to reach legislative compromises that meet the needs of all citizens who make up the single body politic.

By distinguishing clearly the difference between representation and legislation we are able to do greater justice both to the *structural* difference between government and political parties as well as to the *confessional* (worldview) differences among citizens themselves. No group of citizens should be compelled to accommodate itself to the dominant, majoritarian, melting-pot faith simply in order to gain access to electoral representation. Genuine differences of political conviction (whether deeply religious or not) should be allowed to exist and to be held sincerely by citizens (whether grouped in majorities or minorities). Knowing that they would then be represented proportionately, citizens would be free to debate with one another openly without being stifled because their convictions do not fit the contours of an elusive and often shallow majority opinion. Recognizing the structural distinction between political parties (none of which needs to represent a majority, though any one may in fact do so) and representative government thus would make for a more just treatment of the confessionally diverse population that expresses itself in the civic arena.

A pluralist conception of society (in the full structural and confessional sense) differs in fundamental ways from a uniform, melting-pot conception. In a genuinely open society we believe that differences of political viewpoint should be free to contend with one another on the basis of some kind of proportional representation in Congress and state legislatures. It may well be the case that many differences of viewpoint that give birth to political parties in a pluralist society are differences among people who share the same religious outlook on life. On the other hand, there may be differences of a more fundamental character that give birth to distinct political groupings. In a structurally and confessionally diverse society this is as it should be. Citizens ought to be free to associate in political parties as their convictions draw them, and to gain representation proportionate to their numbers.

Political debate that aims merely for majority victory on the basis of a presumed but nonexistent cultural homogeneity is political debate that will not be sufficiently serious to achieve the desired political unity. In fact, evidence suggests that the quality of both electoral debate and governance is degenerating in the United States under the impact of declining party strength, increasing control of elections by special-interest money, and superficial marketing strategies. W. Lance Bennett says that

> The result is a short-circuiting of the public give-and-take in political rituals, such as elections, where candidates and ideas have been tested in the past. As a result, most Americans today experience elections as empty rituals that offer little hope for political dialogue, genuine glimpses of candidate character, or the emergence of a binding consensus on where the nation is going and how it ought to get there.[10]

The government we have today, says George Will,

> is not government by deliberation, it is government by "clout." The test of a faction's clout is its ability to get its appetites translated into government action with maximum speed and minimum alteration. The test is the faction's ability to reduce government, on as many issues as possible, to no more than a recording, ratifying and brokering agency. It is understandable, if not admirable, that factions have this aspiration. What is dismaying is the fact that today's servile government aspires to no higher purposes than those of recording, ratifying and brokering.[11]

Only by means of thorough, critical, moral discourse among citizens, who are free to express genuine convictions in real arguments, will it be possible to build a solid political consensus. Only by finding the means of representing America's diverse citizenry in legislative chambers will it become possible for representatives to practice the art of deliberation and negotiation that will let them rise above the mere recording, ratifying, and brokering of interest-group demands. For this kind of public debate and legislative deliberation to emerge, we believe that both structural and confessional pluralism must be allowed to come into their own.

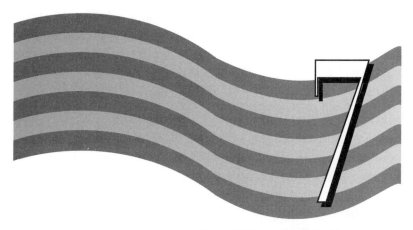

Individual and Institutional Rights

In Sum

Let us begin by recapping the argument of Part II to this point. To emphasize the plural structure of society is, in part, to build on the principle of constitutionally limited government. The jurisdiction of such a government, we believe, should be recognized as limited not merely by the procedural requirements of electoral representation, judicial review, and a constitutional amending process, but chiefly, and in the first place, by the responsibilities that people hold in other God-given relationships and associational competencies such as churches, families, schools, economic enterprises, and various corporate and voluntary organizations. The federal and state governments of the United States should, in fulfillment of their responsibilities, protect and advance the common civic good of American society. All American citizens share a single commonwealth and are subject to the same laws that bind them together in that political community. This is the civic *unum*. However, the single civic community is not omnicompetent over the lives of its citizens as if they constituted a simple, undifferentiated collective called "the people." A just *unum* of citizens under government can flourish only where justice is done to other social and individual competencies—the *pluribus*—held by those same people. Each must be given its proper due.

There is nothing in the Constitution and the common law tradition of the United States that requires American citizens to put their faith in an omnicompetent government or majority will. There is nothing about our constitutional system that requires citizens to pursue an ideal of individual autonomy and liberation from every authority outside civil government. A civic community cannot be built justly on the basis of the mistreatment of society's diverse institutions and relationships. To the contrary, we believe that a constitutionally limited government ought to act in ways that respect both the jurisdictional integrity of nonpolitical organizations and institutions (structural pluralism) as well as the religious freedom of its citizens in all areas of life (confessional pluralism).

All moral discourse about public life, therefore, should be differentiated discourse, which is to say that moral argument ought to distinguish the particular spheres of moral obligation in which people hold different kinds of responsibility. All undifferentiated appeals to justice, goodness, fairness, equality, freedom, correct behavior, or what is good for America, will cause confusion in a differentiated social order. Every appeal that fails to address the persons or institutions responsible for particular kinds of normative behavior will only obfuscate and frustrate the fulfillment of moral responsibility. In the political realm, undifferentiated moral appeals have degenerated into sloganeering contests for control of majority votes (or for Supreme Court rulings) that can compel actions and responses from people without regard to their multiple responsibilities. The tyranny of the majority, which Tocqueville feared, shows many signs of life in countless generalized arguments that are proffered as moral admonitions to people in general—to society at large.

Differentiated public-moral discourse requires the legal and political recognition of both structural and confessional pluralism. Public law is morally legitimate not by virtue of majority vote and constitutionally legitimate procedures alone but only as it does justice to the confessional and institutional diversity of society. Laws are not just if they discriminate against the religious commitments and viewpoints of some citizens by granting special privilege to one above others. Laws cannot be just that contradict or disrupt legitimate responsibilities that people exercise in nongovernmental institutions. Thus, just public laws will be those that give proportionately fair treatment to all religious worldviews expressed in public as well as in private realms of human responsibility.

Pluralism Is Not Relativism

We have been at pains to emphasize that this argument for structural and confessional pluralism is itself part of a *civic-moral* argument for an integrally just state and not an expression of moral relativism. In every arena of life moral norms hold for human behavior and judgment. Truth and error, right and wrong, good and evil, ought to be distinguished in each arena, and people ought to seek the truth and do what is right. In the case of the civic community, the norm of justice obligates government to give proper due to each citizen and to the multiple responsibilities of a complex society as part of its legally integrating responsibility for the commonwealth. Ours, therefore, is a moral argument for a just republic and for the truth of structural and confessional pluralism as an integral part of such a republic in God's creation.

If it were the intent of this book to make the case for true theology, or for sound education, or for healthy sexuality, or for loving family life, or for stewardly business practice, we would be obligated to engage in arguments fit for those realms of life and thought. Not every theology, curriculum, sexual practice, family structure, or business practice is morally legitimate in our view. In each of these arenas of human responsibility, people will and ought to contend for what is true and good.

Our aim here, however, is limited to the quest for clarity about what is normative for the arena of law and politics. And the argument we wish to test by means of rigorous public debate is this: Is it not true that a rightly ordered political community is one in which government and courts exercise an authority of limited, public-legal competence comporting with the norm of public justice for a differentiated society? Public justice, in this respect, calls government to the positive, integrating task of nurturing a healthy commonwealth—a task that simultaneously prohibits it from exercising an undifferentiated, omni-competent authority that would, in effect, allow it to displace or super-sede parental, ecclesiastical, educational, and other independent responsibilities by means of a political/legal authoritarianism. To say it in another way, the *moral good* that constitutional government ought to accomplish is to bind citizens together under law in a civic com-munity of justice that assures to every citizen equal and fair protec-tion. And to be just, that equality *must* express itself both in propor-tionately fair treatment of citizens' diverse religious ways of life as well as in the recognition of their personal and institutional competencies beyond the civic/legal sphere.

This is an argument for a definite kind of political/legal fairness and equity, not an argument for neutrality or relativism. Every political/legal system necessarily imposes an order that excludes alternative political systems. When we say that a state's jurisdiction should be limited and ought to recognize other spheres of competent authority, we do not mean to suggest that two different political/legal systems can share jurisdiction over the same territory. There can be only one system of government in a territory. But it makes all the difference in the world what kind of system it is. A genuinely pluralist constitution cannot exist side by side in the same territory with a nonpluralist constitu-tion. Just as the disestablishment of the church meant the partial dis-placement of one type of political order by another, so the disestab-lishment of government-run schools by a genuinely pluralist system will mean the partial displacement of one type of political order by another. Constitutionally protected pluralism (both confessional and structural) is just as much an imposition as is constitutionally pro-tected majoritarianism or authoritarianism. Our argument is simply that the legal imposition of structural and confessional pluralism sat-isfies the norm of justice for a differentiated society in a way that undif-ferentiated, omnicompetent majoritarianism or authoritarianism can-not do.

The *unum* that ought to be sought in a republic, then, is a properly limited civic/legal unity that binds citizens together in support of con-fessional and structural pluralism. This is what all citizens should enjoy together as part of their equitable participation in the *common*wealth. The political *unum* should not be defined or coerced on the basis of an extralegal or extrapolitical cultural uniformity (whether ecclesiastical, ideological, racial, or something else). Political unity needs to be fashioned on the basis of public justice for all citizens. And the only way to assure a civic/legal unity that does not hang illegitimately on the coattails of an unjust ecclesiastical, ideological, or racial establishment is to make sure that every citizen enjoys full religious freedom in all spheres of life and that government does not overstep the boundaries of its jurisdiction by trying to exercise the authority that belongs to nonpolitical institutions and relationships of society.

Will Institutional Rights Conflict with Individual Rights?

Resistance to the idea of institutional rights proposed here has often come from those who fear that it will lead to the exclusion of some citizens from privileges enjoyed by others. Racial and religious discrimination, for example, seem to rear their ugly heads at this juncture. Our argument, to the contrary, aims to provide an even stronger guarantee for the equal treatment of every citizen than can be provided by arguments from individual rights alone.

The basis for recognizing structural pluralism is precisely the *diversity* of human institutions and relationships. No family, church, school, or business enterprise should be allowed to compete with the political community for government authority. For example, to argue that the family ought to be respected in its own jurisdictional integrity and given public-legal recognition as an institution is not to imply that the family possesses elements of political authority that would entail a grant of political immunity from the state. Both parents and children in a family also remain citizens subject to government's public-legal jurisdiction. Parental authority is not a form of political sovereignty in the home that would, for example, give parents the right to determine whether their children live or die. The very differentiation of public-legal responsibility from parental responsibility is part of what it means to recognize societal differences. Political authority remains unified, touching every citizen; family authority remains multiple and tied to the limits of particular families, none of which, in its own integrity, has authority over any other.

At the same time, however, our argument stresses the fact that citizens are always more than citizens. Government must not treat people as if they may be subject in all respects to public-legal disposition. The just treatment of citizens by government entails the just treatment of various nonpolitical institutions and relationships in which those same people find themselves.

Take another example. Religious exclusion or discrimination should not be permitted by public law. But what does civic equality and nondiscrimination mean for religious citizens? It should mean freedom for them to exercise their religions in mutually exclusive ways. Thus, for a Presbyterian church to insist on the right to hire only a Presbyterian pastor does not mean employment discrimination against Baptists, Jews, Muslims, and atheists. The *civic* rights of Baptists, Jews, Muslims, and atheists are protected by assuring them of the same *public freedom of association* as Presbyterians enjoy. People, in other words, do not exist under the jurisdiction of only one, undifferentiated body of law. Rather, as citizens, they fall under a body of *public* laws that, if just, will recognize the authority of ecclesiastical laws, family rules, and other bodies of law appropriate to particular nonpolitical institutions and relationships. A conflict in public law would arise only if, for example, one ecclesiastical institution were somehow allowed to gain a *public-legal* privilege granted by the state's jurisdiction. This is precisely the problem of injustice with an established church where public privilege is granted to only one church. Even greater injustice existed when members of a particular church were the only ones allowed to hold citizenship in the state. The answer to this error is to distinguish the civil-legal responsibility of the political order from that of the ecclesiastical order and then to treat all citizens equitably and fairly with respect to their diverse and independent ecclesiastical affiliations. Where no public monopoly is allowed, freedom for ecclesiastical association and exclusivity can be just.

But what about employment and commerce? Here the question comes back again to the identities of differentiated institutions. To the extent that an industrial or commercial enterprise exists for the purpose of competing in an open market for its market share of product sales or service, it will be justified in using hiring practices that exclude those unqualified to perform the work required. But an enterprise of this sort typically has no reason (nor should it have any public-legal grant of right) to exclude or fire people for reasons unrelated to the business' purpose and qualifications. By contrast, a women's poetry magazine has every right to hire only a woman editor. A Polish cultural club has every right to hire only a Pole as director. An African-American jazz band has every right to exclude qualified musicians of another race. But in every case, laws against public monopoly and exclusive privilege—which amount to rules that differentiate business responsibilities from those of government—must also exist. African-American jazz bands should not be granted a public privilege that would allow them to outlaw all jazz bands that are not African-American. Women's poetry magazines must not be allowed to use public-legal clout to win for their publications tax support that is denied to men's poetry magazines. Equal protection of every citizen means freedom of association for citizens who will always be more than citizens. They will be poets, restaurant owners, musicians, and manufacturers—organizing to pursue many different kinds of nongovernmental objectives, each of which should be permitted nonmonopolistic exclusiveness according to its own purposes.

Considering this range of issues from the viewpoint of the public trust, we must also make the concomitant point that government (or a majority of citizens acting through government) will never succeed in doing justice if they coopt or incorporate nongovernmental realms of responsibility into state jurisdiction. Schooling is the most critical contemporary issue of dispute in this regard, and we will turn to it again in Chapter 9. The point is that the equal protection of all citizens cannot be achieved if government does injustice to nongovernmental realms of human life by subsuming them under its own bureaucracies.

What about Racism?

One of the especially reprehensible facts of American history has been the treatment of African-American peoples whose ancestors were brought by force to this country to serve as slaves. The beginning of the injustice was to reduce African peoples to a "group" identity based essentially on skin color, thus violating both the identity of human personhood as well as the differentiated responsibilities that these people should have been allowed to enjoy. Slaves were treated as a class of property that permitted no legal protection of their marriages, families, or any other personal or institutional responsibilities they had. To define a "group" of people in this fashion is to violate every principle for which we have been arguing.

From our point of view, an undifferentiated "group" does not exist in a differentiated society. The only universal (though not exhaustive) category is that of citizen, but citizens do not constitute an undifferentiated group. Citizenship by its very nature means membership in the *political* community, which has its own specific, differentiated character, authority structure, duties, rights, functions, and privileges. Beyond citizenship in the state, there exist many different relationships and institutions in which human beings ought to have the politically protected right to participate—marriages, families, schools, various places of employment, churches, and the electoral process. None of these, not even the political community, is an undifferentiated group.

When slavery was constitutionally outlawed after the Civil War, African Americans should have been able to enter into the full protection of the law, which would have meant that "blackness" would no longer have any meaning as a qualification for civic identity. Former slaves, who had special economic and social needs, should have been helped by means of particular legislation to provide special assistance until they could become educated, propertied, and otherwise self-sufficient citizens. And equally important, they should have been allowed to participate in an electoral process characterized by proportional representation. Hypothetically, after a generation or two of such recovery, black-skinned Americans should have been as independent as English, French, Chinese, and Mexican Americans, enjoying full rights of citizenship in a differentiated society of diverse nongovernmental responsibilities.

We know, tragically, that this was not the course taken in American history. One consequence has been that many black as well as many white Americans have continued to hold on to inappropriate "group" identities that only further aggravate past injustices. The civil rights movement properly sought to put an end to all legal discrimination against African Americans on the basis of racial identity. In other words, it sought to eliminate all remaining vestiges of laws that allowed for the treatment (usually maltreatment) of black Americans as a group defined by skin color. This was as it should be.

Once all legal discrimination has ended, however (and we are not suggesting that none whatever remains), public justice requires that all citizens be treated without discrimination in accord with the principles outlined above. This means, among other things, that African Americans should not now be identified as an undifferentiated "group" for purposes of special, affirmative legislation and constitutional recognition. This is, in part, the burden of the argument by Shelby Steele who exposes and bemoans the continuing power of illegitimate group identities that were fashioned out of earlier injustices.[1] The tragedy for African Americans, according to Steele, is that the pain of past victimization remains so real that many people continue to use it as a means of advocating an approach to politics that feeds on that earlier undifferentiated group identity—the group as victim. Steele's analysis of the contemporary American situation points precisely to the need for societal differentiation that overcomes mistaken, undifferentiated moralism:

> The exaggeration of black victimization is always the first indication that a current event is being transformed by mistrust into a subjective correlative that sanctions the pursuit of racial power. (As discussed in the first chapter of this book, victimization is a form of innocence and innocence always entitles us to pursue power.) The current black leadership has injured its credibility by its tendency to make so many black problems into correlatives for black oppression. The epidemic of black teen pregnancies, the weakened black family, the decline in the number of black college students, and so on are too often cast as correlatives of historic racism. . . . Such claims are exaggerations because racism simply does not fully explain these problems. No doubt they have something to do with the historic wounds of oppression, but what the charge of racism does not explain is the giving in to these wounds more than ever before during a twenty-five-year decline in racism and discrimination.[2]

What Steele's argument does not do adequately, however, is recognize the need for the protection of structural and confessional pluralism in society, including proportional representation in the electoral process. In opposition to the misidentification of a race as a collective whole, Steele emphasizes only the rights, opportunities, and responsibilities of individuals. Steele says of black Americans: "There will be no end to despair and no lasting solution to any of our problems until we rely on individual effort within the American mainstream—rather than collective action against the mainstream—as our means of advancement."[3] Inversion, in the sense of the use of a negative past for positive contemporary purposes, says Steele, "draws us back into a preoccupation with our collective identity at the very moment when we most stand to gain from the initiative of individuals who are unburdened by too much collective obligation."[4] "As individuals," Steele writes,

> blacks cannot help but want the same sorts of things all individuals want, namely, a better life—an education, a home, a prosperous career, a well-cared-for family, maybe fame and wealth. But the pursuit of these things will inevitably draw us into the American mainstream where we will surely encounter much racial vulnerability.[5]

The problem with this argument, from our point of view, is that society is not composed merely of individuals any more than it is composed of undifferentiated ethnic "groups" or other collectives. The "American mainstream" (itself a highly undifferentiated phrase) to which Steele refers has in the past been defined and controlled in its political, economic, and educational history by a majority culture that has not always done justice to the diversity of cultures, confessions, institutions, and relationships in American society. The rejection of racial groupings, therefore, is not sufficient to assure individuals fair treatment under the law. The question is whether all citizens can experience equal treatment in rearing their families, choosing schools for their children, practicing their religions, enjoying cultural solidarity as they freely choose it, gaining access to the market for employment, and gaining political representation.[6]

Arthur Schlesinger's appeal to history similarly misses the point we want to make, namely, that the American nation should *not* be defined by an undifferentiated and legally privileged "mainstream." He correctly emphasizes that the teaching of history should not be degraded "by allowing its contents to be dictated by pressure groups, whether political, economic, religious, or ethnic."[7] But he fails to make the equally important point that different views of history ought not to be squelched by political authorities in the name of political, economic, religious, or ethnic uniformity.

Schlesinger's oversight is due to his precommitment to an idea of the American nation that is every bit as undifferentiated as the mythical black collective that Steele wishes to reject. "The American Creed," Schlesinger writes, "envisages a nation composed of individuals making their own choices and accountable to themselves, not a nation based on inviolable ethnic communities. The Constitution turns on individual rights, not on group rights."[8] This may be the creed that

Schlesinger holds, but what about those Americans who hold a more differentiated view of the United States and who therefore may wish to teach history and even interpret the Constitution from a different point of view? Should a majority of Americans as a "group" have the political right to determine for all citizens the "true" meaning of history, the correct curricula of schools, and the proper meaning of America's mainstream culture? History, says Schlesinger,

> can give a sense of national identity. We don't have to believe that our values are absolutely better than the next fellow's or the next country's, but we have no doubt that they are better *for us*, reared as we are—and are worth living by and worth dying for. For our values are not matters of whim and happenstance. History has given them to us. They are anchored in our national experience, in our great national documents, in our national heroes, in our folkways, traditions, and standards. People with a different history have differing values. But we believe that our own are better for us.[9]

Who is the "we" to whom Schlesinger refers here? Does he truly believe that if history and values can be different for people of different countries, they will not be different among diverse peoples living in the same country? Must we really insist that every hero in American history is one whom African Americans, Hispanic Americans, European Americans, and Asian Americans will all treasure? Must the political decisions of the majority determine the meaning of public life for all Americans? Schlesinger's individualism fits hand in glove with his undifferentiated nationalism. Together, these two poles of his thought lead him to ignore the plural structure and plural confessions of society—or at least to push them off into private corners. His religiously deep liberalism keeps him from recognizing the overwhelming and often detrimental power that the majority culture has exerted on minorities in American society.

We agree with Steele that black individuals in the United States today have more opportunity than ever before and that racial discrimination is no longer legal. But many citizens (whether black or of any other color) who want to pursue education, family life, and social service, or who wish to seek a career in business or representation in government, may find that if they try to do these things in ways different from those that Schlesinger finds acceptable, they will very likely meet obstacles—some of them fundamentally unjust. It is one thing to ask individual African Americans (or citizens of any other racial or cultural identity) to cast aside their sense of group victimization and to accept courageously their responsibilities as free citizens. It is quite another to ask them to allow an equally undifferentiated but majoritarian mainstream to define the context within which—as individuals—they must rear and educate their children, define their religion, pursue their careers, and be represented politically. We must make room in American society for freely chosen minority expressions. This is not a call for recognizing mythical and closed group identities based on skin color, gender, or ideology—and it is certainly not to encourage group identity based on a sense of victimization. It *is*, instead, a call for the public-legal recognition of diverse schools, publications, families, friendships, businesses, voluntary agencies, and political parties—any number of which might manifest the free associational allegiances of self-identified numerical minorities in American society. There should be room here for many kinds of people to live in diverse ways in a single political order.

As Stephen Carter puts it, challenging Shelby Steele: a sense of ethnic or racial solidarity need not mean

> embracing some special perspective gained from our [African-American] history of oppression; nor need it mean . . . suppressing dissent; it means, rather, embracing our people themselves, in all their wild and frustrating variety.
>
> Embracing our people does not mean suspending judgment. . . . [J]udgment is not inconsistent with solidarity, not in the positive, loving, embracing sense of the word. And professional attainment is not inconsistent with it, either. To be middle class, financially secure, suburbanite, need not mean, if one is black, to be fully assimilated. It *does* make a difference when I decide whether to move into a neighborhood that I see other black people there. It *does* make a difference to me that my children have black playmates, that they regularly interact with black adults other than their own parents. It *does* make a difference to me that I not be the only black, the first black, the best black. Alice Walker is right: the civil rights movement's greatest gift to my generation, and to generations to come, is not simply the opportunity to set goals that were denied, often by law, to our parents and theirs but also—and perhaps more important—the brimming confidence that solidarity breeds. Not solidarity in the sense of groupness, but solidarity in the sense of valuing one another.[10]

To be an American citizen—to enjoy both solidarity with all citizens in a just republic as well as the legal protection of one's individual and institutional rights—should also mean being free to value one's ethnic or religious heritage in a special way without being marginalized simply because one is not part of a majority culture or religion. Only by means of structural and confessional pluralism can such freedom be achieved and sustained.

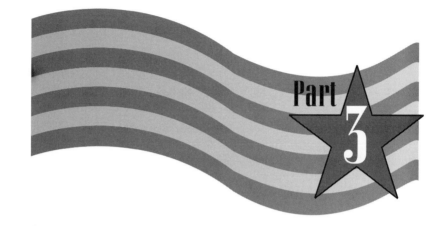

Reforming the American Polity

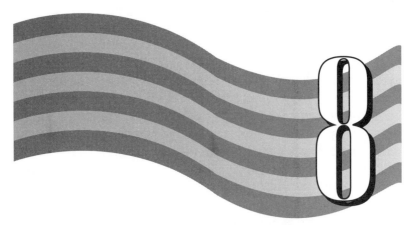

Exercising Religious Freedom

What is the authoritative American tradition regarding the relation of religion to public life? The United States is a Christian nation, some say, while others insist that the country's distinctive identity is to be found in its secular neutrality made possible by the separation of church and state. "Religious freedom" is the key phrase for many; "separation" is the preeminent word for others.

Depending on how citizens interpret tradition, and depending on what they consider to be authoritative in that tradition, they often walk along different paths through contemporary American politics. There may be no clearer illustration of the influence of religiously rooted views of life than in the contrasting interpretations of the First Amendment. Nearly everyone in the country believes in the mutual independence of church and state. Few if any argue for the national establishment of a particular church or for an ecclesiastical takeover of the federal government. But that is only a small part of what the First Amendment debate is all about. The larger question concerns the nature of religion, not just the relation of organized churches to government.

The Authority of the Moral Republican Tradition

From one historic point of view the First Amendment serves as a means not only of removing religious warfare from politics but also of opening the way to a common moral basis for public life once the latter has been liberated from religious conflict. Thomas Jefferson held such a view. To be sure, Jefferson was a religious person—a deist whose moral convictions were closely tied to his religious faith. But Jefferson helped shape a tradition of political morality in which the word "religion" increasingly came to be used only with reference to those convictions, opinions, and ecclesiastical institutions that he considered to be parochially peculiar and not publicly universal. Any such parochial conviction or institution has value insofar as its morality overlaps with, and helps reinforce, the universal morality needed for common life in the Republic. Anything that remains parochial or peculiar, such as distinctive theological convictions, should be confined, Jefferson thought, to a private sphere where it will not disrupt the common, rational process of shaping a majority consensus in the practice of self-government. Jefferson considered his own faith and vision of life to be universal and not parochial.[1]

Insofar as one accepts Jefferson's distinction between a universal moral sense of what is right for public life, on the one hand, and the parochial character of distinct rites, confessions, dogmas, and theologies, on the other hand, one is firmly positioned to use the familiar language that gradually emerged from that view of life: a "nonsectarian" public sphere contrasts with the private "sectarian" sphere; secular government exists over against parochial religious institutions; the state performs nonsectarian functions in contrast to the sectarian activities of organized religions; and a universal rational morality stands in contrast to multiple sectarian dogmas.[2]

But note how this worldview, taken as a whole, locates the distinction between state and church within a larger framework—the framework of an enlightened, moralistic religion. This cannot be seen so easily from within the Jeffersonian standpoint because, from that point of view, "religion" has, by gradual redefinition, come to be regarded as a private, parochial matter. Once religion has been equated with the church and a sectarian realm, it is difficult to recognize the thoroughly religious character of the comprehensive worldview that creates the distinction between religion and secular, between the sectarian and the nonsectarian. But if we step back and ask about the character of that framework as a whole, we can see something quite different.

Jefferson recognized to some extent that his own deepest faith—a view of life that supported the distinction between the universal and the sectarian, between the commonly moral and the parochially ecclesiastical—was a religion. Whether or not one believes that God exists, according to Jefferson (and he did hold such a belief), human beings owe it to their common moral sense not only to seek personal goodness through disciplined labor and learning but also to help build a republic through which they might realize their highest, common moral purpose.[3] Jefferson envisioned a new kind of moral/religious community arising in the future on the ash heap of discarded ignorance, superstition, and subservience to priests and aristocrats. He expected theological and other dogmatic parochialisms to atrophy and drop away as human beings stepped up to the wider, higher plain of a rational, unitarian republic of free citizens.

Jefferson confessed this faith (which combined Renaissance-revived Stoicism, Christianity, and early modern rationalism) as a comprehensive vision that should (*ought to*) displace the worldview prevalent in his day. He hoped that traditional religious views of life and politics would give way to this new vision so that a solid republic of conscientiously free citizens could be built. The fact that Jefferson believed traditional religious institutions should be given freedom in a private sphere (separated from any control of, or privileged position in, political life) meant that his view of life was tolerant enough to accommodate those who were still dependent on older faiths. But Jefferson's tolerance of worldviews different from his own was tied to his hope that parochial religions would remain private. Only one view of life, only one philosophy, only one moral consensus could successfully supply the Republic with the glue needed to bind it together free of sectarian conflict. For all practical purposes Jefferson envisioned an undifferentiated though limited civic-moral community.

This comprehensive view of life (modified over the years by a variety of other influences) gradually gained dominance as a civil religion and public philosophy in the United States. Enlightenment rationalists, romantic nationalists, and those whom today we might call secular humanists were not the only ones to accept the authority of this tradition. This view of life also took hold among many people who continued to identify themselves as orthodox Protestants, Catholics, and Jews. Increasingly they came to view their own denominational and theological religions as private, personal, and ecclesiastical, and to view the public sphere through the glasses of the dominant civil religion.[4] The United States, as a civic community, should be governed, most came to believe, by the majority acting through a process of common, moral consensus-building without interference from parochial religious convictions. Many if not most of our contemporaries now interpret the First Amendment to mean that citizens in public life should be protected *from* religion. Michael McConnell summarizes the point this way:

> Substituting [Jefferson's] so-called "wall of separation" and other misleading metaphors for the language of the Constitution, many government officials and courts have transmuted the principle of freedom of religion into a rigid doctrine that everything in the public sphere must be secular—in effect, replacing the ideals of pluralism and neutrality with the quite different ideals of secularism and separation. In an opinion in one recent case, Justice Harry A. Blackmun went so far as to use the term "secular liberty" as his description of what the religion clauses are all about. This is what I call freedom from religion.[5]

Of course, this belief that a nonsectarian, "secular," moral consensus should hold for public life is not itself neutral or free from its own religiously deep presuppositions. It merely hides from view its own thoroughly parochial and often discriminatory features. The dominant moral consensus throughout most of American history was, after all, largely Protestant, and it rose to heights of extreme intolerance against immigrating Catholics in the nineteenth century. In its increasingly secularized version—à la John Dewey and others—this new religion of moral, democratic universality even fueled popular hopes of an American century in which the rest of the world (obviously the majority at the time) would come to recognize the universal truth already discovered by and embodied in the small, avant-garde American experiment.

Telling the story of the emergence of an American civil religion, Sidney Mead suggests that this nation "conceived in liberty and dedicated to the proposition that all men are created equal" is a "nation with the soul of a church" whose "spiritual core" is "theonomous cosmopolitanism."

As the Christian sects [of the early American Republic] carried the universal vision until it was, largely in spite of them, incarnated in a religiously pluralistic commonwealth, so perhaps that commonwealth is the bearer in history of the cosmopolitanism which, when and if incarnated in world institutions, may compel the nation-churches to live side by side in overt peace under law—as our Republic compelled the heteronomous religious sects to do until they discovered that limitation of their conflicts to reason and persuasion was a viable path to peace and union—that dialogue was a virtue.[6]

The point we want to make is that this cosmopolitan worldview, according to which a supposedly nonsectarian and rational morality enables the nation to tolerate so-called sectarian differences in private, is itself a thoroughly *religious* view of life. It is no less "sectarian" (in the sense of being dependent on a faith that lacks universality and self-evidency) than is the Christian/classical worldview that gained political dominance in the Middle Ages. But in gaining the ascendancy in American law and politics, this enlightened, republican moralism redefined the terms of public discourse in a way that managed to disguise its own religious nature while putting all other religions in the box of private, sectarian parochialism.

This dominant view of public and private life still carries moral weight with many Christians and Jews insofar as they believe that the common morality of the public realm is generally coincident with their own deepest convictions about the terms on which public life ought to be conducted. In other words, they may not share all of Jefferson's deistic theological convictions but they accept his public/parochial, nonsectarian/sectarian distinction as the best way to comprehend the relation of politics to religion and of state to church.

The question today, however, is whether this long-standing, Enlightenment-rooted worldview is not losing its majoritarian grip. A growing number of citizens no longer believe that the Jeffersonian worldview is universal, common, neutral, or nonsectarian. Many Protestants are waking up to the fact that their once dominant public moral consensus is no longer regarded as universal and may not be upheld much longer by the majority. Newer religions are increasingly in evidence, and not all of their adherents want to keep their deepest convictions closeted in a private, parochial space. Many traditional Christians and Jews are beginning to insist that their religions ought not to be arbitrarily confined to a narrow sphere outside the political and legal arena.[7] Some even realize that their comprehensive religious approach to life may conflict at root with the comprehensive civil religion of Enlightenment and post-Enlightenment humanism. The crisis emerging at America's political foundations is thus, in part, a religious crisis because the American political order has, from the beginning, been shaped by competing religious worldviews.

The Religious Freedom Tradition

Consider now a contrasting view of religion and its relation to public life—a view grounded in presuppositions different from those of Jefferson and his heirs. One may argue with equal accuracy, we believe, that the late eighteenth-century refusal to establish a church in the new federal system had nothing necessarily to do with Jefferson's interpretation of the First Amendment. The aim to prohibit the government's privileging of one religion over another was to codify the newly emerging conviction that government should be limited in its authority over the lives of its citizens. Freedom of conscience in all of life, including politics, should be a constitutional precondition of government's authority over the civic community. Religious freedom is an essential, normative principle for human life and sets one of the prior boundaries for the civic community whose government ought not to exercise omnicompetent authority. A state without an established religion is a state in which the free exercise of religion allows citizens to live out their faiths, to practice their religions freely. The separation of church from state—or, better said, the disestablishment of the church—is not at all the same as separating religion from politics. One may not presume, as Jefferson did, that a common, public morality will or should arise to displace religious differences in the public sphere.

What the First Amendment helps make possible is a state in which citizens are liberated from legally discriminatory prejudice against their religious (and other) convictions, and on that basis they are also free to contend with one another by the peaceful means of elections, legislation, and judicial proceedings in the shaping of a common, limited, civic polity. What they are no longer permitted to do as citizens is to conduct winner-take-all battles aimed at establishing a single religion. Different churches should all be treated with the same public deference and equal protection, but likewise the diversity of religions (functioning both inside and outside churches) should each receive equally fair and nondiscriminatory treatment so that citizens may live out their faiths in family life, education, and the political debates that shape public policy. The true nature of religious freedom means that the state has no right to *pre*determine or *pre*define the nature and limits of religion. The First Amendment does not define religion as private, parochial, sectarian, and nonpolitical; rather, the First Amendment has as its purpose to set limits to both federal and state governments with regard to their authority to address the exercise of religious freedom.

From this alternative point of view, religious life can be recognized as having more than a private, parochial character. Jefferson's (or Dewey's or Justice Blackmun's) deepest and most comprehensive view of life can now be recognized for what it really is, namely, one religious outlook among others. Churches certainly are religious and ought to be respected by the State as independent institutions. But the diversity of religions ought not to be confined by legal dictate to only one sphere of life, namely, to churches. The very nature of a religion is that it orients and controls people's approaches to all of life, including politics. Religions are deeper and more encompassing than the institutional spheres of church and state. The only way, therefore, to protect religious freedom is to restrict political authority to the responsibility, among other things, of protecting all religions equally. Citizens with diverse points of view and approaches to life should be equally free to practice their faiths and to seek through constitutional means a quality of civic life that can serve them all fairly.

According to McConnell, the groups that first agitated for the addition of the free exercise and establishment clauses of the First Amendment wanted both freedom *from* and freedom *for* religious faith.

> They believed true piety to be the product of a free and unfettered conscience, which meant that there must be a freedom from religion because there cannot be a free and unfettered conscience to accept religion without there also being a free and unfettered conscience to reject religion. . . . But they did not intend to create a society in which religion was driven underground, where secular ideologies are given a privileged position. They did not intend a society in which the full brunt of government power could be used to disadvantage those who did come to the free and unfettered choice to believe and worship God, as they put it, "in the manner and season most agreeable to their consciences."[8]

From this standpoint, a limited republic that protects the religious freedom of its citizens is something quite different from an undifferentiated, one-willed human community. It is different from the universal moral community that Jefferson and others envisioned. Rather, the political community should be recognized here as a specific public-legal trust held in common by all citizens—by citizens who also happen to be more than citizens and who also happen to live by different faiths. To be sure, civic life in a republic demands vigorous cooperation among those who hold divergent views of life as they seek to build a common legal system and to legislate policies that will bind them together in justice. Though difficult to achieve, a common *civic* bond is not out of the question, even in face of deep religious differences. But the civic bond must *not* be allowed to expand in an undifferentiated fashion to become a total community that disregards other communities and institutions of society. Government of the American Republic is not supposed to privilege one religion or another by confining all nonmajoritarian faiths to parochial privacy.

What is becoming most divisive in American public life is the insistence of some citizens (perhaps the majority) that they are morally justified in using legal and political means to establish as the only common basis for the civic order a viewpoint that pretends to be religiously neutral and capable of setting religious differences aside. That approach amounts to nothing less than a majority power play, allowing the religiously deep views of the majority to dictate the terms of moral discourse, of legal and political decision-making in the public square.

Justice for Religions

The chief political and constitutional questions in dispute today are no longer typically about a church establishment or the relative independence of churches in society. What *is* in dispute is whether citizens are free to practice their religions (both inside and outside churches) with the assurance of fair and equal protection under the law. These disputes, we believe, will not be settled as long as public law defines religion narrowly and confines most religious expressions to a private sphere while giving majoritarian control to an equally religious view of life that escapes the tag "parochial" by virtue of its self-designation as secular or nonsectarian.

Just as the founders of the early federal Republic decided to disestablish the church in order to obtain an independent, more clearly defined, and more just *civic* community, so today we believe that the United States needs to disestablish the dominant civil religion that shapes society by means of the bipolar dichotomy of sacred/secular, nonsectarian/sectarian, rationally neutral/religiously biased. The way to resolve religiously deep disputes about public life is not to grant a privilege to secularism in public life while pushing other views of life out of the public arena, but rather to assure all religions equal access to the public square regardless of their majority or minority status.

What we have called the Jeffersonian tradition, but which is much broader than that, has contributed relatively little to the clarification of the civic community's unique identity (in differentiation from the identities of other kinds of institutions and communities) because it continues to uphold the ideal of an undifferentiated moral-cultural consensus as the necessary binding glue of the Republic. As long as people accept the authority of this faith, they will inevitably interpret America's expanding religious and cultural pluralism as a threat to the Republic's stability. But if Americans will learn to distinguish their civic bond from deeper cultural and religious bonds, they may be able to find a path that leads to the strengthening of their civic bonds by way of doing greater justice to the diversity of their religious convictions and ways of life.

One of the weaknesses of James Hunter's "culture wars" analysis is that he does not give sufficient attention to the character of this civic bond that structures most of the conflicts he dissects. Thus, he reads too much into the bipolarity of many conflicts because he sees them all as signs of a fundamental religiocultural division when, in fact, many of them are forced on citizens by the all-or-nothing, winner-take-all character of political and legal processes. When Hunter comes to suggest ways for Americans to overcome their growing polarization, he expresses the hope that a new "public philosophy" might be adopted by these culturally divided people (or by a majority of them, at least). But this raises the question: How will those who are so deeply divided culturally be able to arrive at a publicly significant common philosophy? Given Hunter's assessment of the cultural crisis, it is hard to imagine that anything like a common public philosophy could emerge. Such a philosophy would have to succeed, for example, in clarifying the nature and limits of political unity in relation to religious and social diversity. It would have to be a specifically political and legal philosophy, not merely a new variation on the old civil-religious theme of undifferentiated moralism.

But Hunter does not move unambiguously in that direction; he sticks with the hope of recovering a more general moral consensus that will supply the unity sufficient to sustain cooperation within the existing political and legal processes. "Cultural conflict," he says, (though he should have said "political conflict")

> may be about the struggle for domination, but the conflict can be channeled and made equitable through the creation and institutionalization of a relatively autonomous public philosophy. *Agreement around a renewed public philosophy could establish a context of public discourse, not to mention the legal and political apparatus, to sustain a genuine and peaceable pluralism—even in the face of what appears to be the monumental compulsion of history.*[9]

How is a "relatively autonomous" philosophy to be established apart from the seemingly all-pervasive cultural divisions? If the political arena has become the chief context of cultural warfare, how does Hunter imagine that an agreement can be established ahead of time to channel those divisions into relatively equitable and peaceable controversy? What would the new (if it is to be new) "legal and political apparatus" look like? The evidence suggests that Hunter is still under the sway of Jefferson and Dewey, whose hope was that a nonsectarian public philosophy would come to the rescue of culturally and religiously divided citizens. But that is precisely the error of faith that ought to be exposed. Every cultural, philosophical, political idea of public unity is grounded in a religiously deep point of view. There is no nonsectarian standpoint that will allow people to "channel" their otherwise deep differences into a neutral settlement. What we need instead is an argument—acknowledging its own religiously deep roots—which shows the kind of *political-legal* order (apparatus) that *can* do justice to cultural and religious diversity. If religiously deep cultural differences are real, then an appeal for a public philosophy that unites people at a level *deeper* than their religious differences is a mythical appeal that is internally contradictory. This religiously powerful myth has, nonetheless, fueled civil-religious nationalism for more than a century.

This is why the people most likely to resist the legalization of greater religious pluralism are those whose religion is the civil religion of the American Republic. These are the people who believe that somehow their own convictions represent (or ought to represent) the will of the majority and should therefore have exclusive power to shape the secular public square for all citizens. This viewpoint pushes strongly in the direction of supporting the majority's right to an undifferentiated control of public life. Whether or not minority viewpoints arise from deeply held religious convictions or from racial identity or from other human characteristics, the legal/political pressure from political majoritarians inevitably makes minorities feel like second-class or excluded citizens. Typically, those who feel excluded or mistreated will respond by making demands for their rights so that the ruling consensus can be revised to give them the same undifferentiated access and public privileges that the majority enjoys. But within a winner-take-all framework of this kind, politics and legal proceedings degenerate into a struggle among everyone for the power to define a single, dominant consensus. The aim then becomes not equitable justice for diverse views and approaches to life but rather a perpetual revising of the "authoritative" majority consensus for purposes of society-wide political power. Driven by this power struggle, the shaping of the so-called consensus reveals less and less of an actual moral consensus. What the majority is able to produce under these conditions becomes increasingly thin, more confused, and more arbitrary in its exclusion of the viewpoints that still fall outside the dominant "consensus." And any person or group that cannot gain what it wants by having its demands included in the new consensus lives with the fear of losing everything. That fear, in turn, heightens tension and may fuel increasingly desperate tactics in the battle for political control.

The present crisis in American law and politics may have arisen not so much from the diversifying pluralism of moral and religious viewpoints in American society as from the resistance of the dominant civil religion to changes in the political and legal systems that would serve the country's diverse religions with greater justice. At work, in part, is a dispute among different views of religion and political order. At the same time, since the dominant philosophy operative throughout the history of our Republic has been a largely undifferentiated, civil-religious nationalism, the crisis involves specific political and legal questions about how to order the polity so that justice can be done to the confessional and structural diversity of American society.

We believe that the enlightened, Jeffersonian tradition has reached the point of serious internal crisis and that a different normative conception of a pluralistic society, as articulated in Part II, is needed to make it possible for citizens to build a more just political community. The outcome, perhaps best illustrated by the argument for educational pluralism in the next chapter, will be a growing public recognition of, and sometimes equitable public financial support for, diverse approaches in all spheres of life. Social services, health care, broadcasting, schooling, job training, and a host of other activities should be recognized as allowing a variety of independent approaches organized by people with diverse views of life. Some schools and hospitals may be self-professedly secular, or Catholic, or Muslim. Some counseling centers, soup kitchens, and nonprofit legal-aid clinics may be Jewish or evangelical. Those that are self-professedly religious should not be treated any differently than those that profess to be secular or that happen to be run by the government. Religious life—whether recognized as traditional or contemporary, whether oriented to the biblical God or to some intramundane principle or ideal—will be free to flourish not only in churches, synagogues, and temples but in all the arenas of public and private life without legal or governmental discrimination.

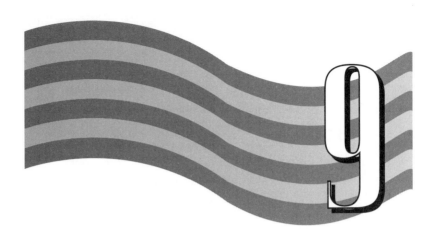

Schooling in the Republic

The majority consensus that has shaped the public laws for American schooling from about the 1840s to the present is a consensus grounded largely in the religiously deep view of life that we have connected with Thomas Jefferson. From this viewpoint, the authoritative tradition for the governance of education reaches back through the Stoics to ancient Greece and is now taken for granted by most citizens as constituting the moral basis for education in our Republic. But that tradition is now in trouble, which helps explain the contemporary crisis of both politics and education in the United States.

Schooling as Civic Training

Schooling, from the viewpoint of the main tradition, is a function of the Republic, and its chief purpose is to mold citizens. As Robert Bellah and his colleagues say, "It is part of our classical heritage to see education at the center of our common life."[1] The moral reasoning involved here does not require the differentiation of school from state. Instead, the common, mutually supportive purpose of both institutions is established along a single line of moral argument. In fact, as we will try to show, a contrary moral argument that urges the differentiation of schools from the state in order to allow for the distinction between political-moral reasoning, on the one hand, and educational-moral reasoning, on the other, challenges the ideal of republican education that Jefferson and others helped create.

In a self-governing republic, as Jefferson saw it, all citizens need to receive sufficient, common training to allow them to become independent, enlightened citizens and rational decision makers. Parochial confinements must be overcome so that no citizen will remain subject to sectarian myths and other irrationalities imposed by aristocrats and priests. A common, governmentally organized system of free schools, Jefferson believed, would be necessary to nurture the common moral sense in every individual and to prepare each person for responsible independence and civic life.

The common school came into existence, therefore, to nurture a universal morality and to train rational minds. A common education became, in effect, the substitute for a common ecclesiastical faith inculcated by an established church. An all-inclusive civic community should, by means of the common school, be able to overcome moral and religious divisions in public life. The formerly authoritative traditions connected with warring religious factions should be replaced by a new public philosophy grounded in universal moral certitude—grounded in self-evident truths—nurtured in each child by rational and moral means. Independent citizens thus enlightened through common republican schooling and subject to governing authorities put in place by their consent would constitute the vital force of a healthy republic. The Bellah team is not the first to point out that one consequence of this ideal of education is the conviction, still held strongly by most Americans today, that American schooling is "something of a secular religion."[2]

Families, from Jefferson's point of view, serve a variety of good purposes, including the provision of love, companionship, apprenticeship, and more. But children should be subject to their parents only insofar as that subjection is compatible with a morally coherent republic built on the ideal of independent citizens commonly schooled and capable of governing themselves. Schooling for citizenship, therefore, is first of all a common public responsibility—not a familial or ecclesiastical responsibility.[3]

Any approach to schooling that remains confined by parochial attachments cannot, by definition, be acceptable as *common* schooling. This is why the fight for the common school, led by Benjamin Rush, Noah Webster, and Horace Mann was, of necessity, a fight for a governmentally organized and financed school system that would be able to transcend the educational authority of parents and churches. As students, children were thought to be citizens of the state more than members of families. Schooling in or by churches, families, or other independent agencies would inevitably reflect the very parochialism that the common school was supposed to overcome. Here the moral argument for public schooling became the argument for a certain kind of republic. In a manner quite parallel to earlier moral arguments in support of an established church, the argument for the common school simply assumed that a stable political order could not be sustained by a diversity of independent schools with different educational philosophies.

Just as Jefferson's public worldview was highly religious in its own unitarian, republican fashion, so his approach to schooling, which became law in the middle of the nineteenth century, was far removed from religious neutrality. Catholic immigrants streaming into Boston and New York in the 1840s confronted a Protestant majority that had finally come to accept Jefferson's and Mann's educational ideals as the means of guarding their republic from sectarian disruption. Catholic families would either have to accept the free education of the common schools and do away with their "parochial" schools or they would, in essence, have to accept the status of second-class citizens if they chose to maintain their Catholic schools at private expense.

For a long time after the 1840s, the so-called nonparochial *public* schools remained thoroughly Protestant, religious, and morally strict. There was nothing secular or neutral about them. As James Hunter says, "the educational establishment rejected public funds for sectarian education yet that establishment itself was thoroughly sectarian, albeit of the dominant Protestant variety."[4] As a reflection of the majority Protestant culture, which happened to have political control, these schools were thought by that majority to be nonsectarian and common. But not all Americans shared that prejudice. Clearly, the battle over schooling in the nineteenth century was not between religious and nonreligious constituencies. Rather the competition was between those, on the one hand, who held the ideal of a republic that enforces common schooling of one variety (moral and religious as that was), and, on the other hand, those who hoped for a republic that could be built on religiously diverse schooling. The ideal of the common school (rooted in the Jeffersonian view of political order) won out, not because it was in fact truly neutral or universal, and certainly not because it was nonreligious, but because its backers—the majority Protestants—held the political power that enabled them to call their schools non-sectarian and to establish schooling as a function of the political community. The political/legal structure of schooling was settled in winner-take-all fashion by means of majority political power that gave a public funding monopoly to government-run schools and confined anything it deemed parochial to the same private sidelines where it confined nonmajoritarian religions.

Note that pluralism or diversity in education must, from this viewpoint, be restricted to a nonpublic sphere. The moral argument is not first of all about the content of education but about the identity of a republican community. For such a community to exist, Jefferson and others believed, it must have a common (at least majority) moral commitment to certain republican/democratic principles of individual freedom and self-government that supposedly emerge only (or best) from common schooling. For the authorities to support diverse kinds of schooling would obviously be to invite a threat to the Republic as serious as any that would arise from allowing children not to be educated at all or allowing a minority to rule.

What is of concern to us here is not the ongoing, internal disputes (both political and pedagogical) over the curricula in what are now called "public" schools. Rather, our chief interest is in the political and legal structure that has been established for schooling. Nothing about this system of schooling was presupposed by or written into the constitutional settlement of 1787. Nevertheless, it eventually grew to become the authoritative American tradition.

Schooling as Extension of Parental Responsibility

An alternate view of the place of education in the Republic, though sidelined after the 1840s, has continued to influence and to expose ambiguities in the now-dominant legal framework of American education. From this second point of view, schooling (at least for minor children) is seen first of all, though not exclusively, as an extension of the family's child-rearing responsibilities. Schooling serves many purposes, including training for employment, moral discipline, and religious instruction, as well as civic training. Insofar as families have different views of life and different expectations for their children's future they ought to be free to choose schooling that is consonant with their religiously deep convictions as well as with their civic obligations. In other words, parents, not the state, should be recognized as the *principal* party responsible for the education of young children, and public justice can be done to parents and children only if full legal respect is granted to families in their diverse religious, cultural, and moral traditions.

Commitment to, and preparation for, a common civic life no more depends on or requires uniform, government-run schools for all children than it depends on or requires an established church. The governmental interest in civic training for self-governing citizens can be achieved by means of the legal requirement that (for example) every child should learn so much English, history, and civics in any setting where education takes place. For the sake of civic equity, government certainly may (and perhaps should) fund elementary and secondary schooling by means of public taxation. To do justice to parents and schools, however, those funds should be distributed equitably to *all* children wherever they receive their schooling.

From this alternate viewpoint, since schooling is, first of all, an extension of child rearing and not merely or chiefly a means of civic training, government's legitimate concern with civic well-being must be expressed in keeping with the just treatment of families, society's foundation stones. Ultimately it is parents who should be held accountable for rearing their children responsibly. Governments do not need to own and operate all (or any) of the schools they fund in order to assure that children receive an education that includes civic training. Moreover, the equitable support of a variety of schools reflecting the diverse moral, cultural, and religious views of the citizenry can be a means of *solidifying* support from all citizens for government's educational responsibility. Whether parents choose schools run by churches or by independent boards, schools shaped by a Christian faith or by agnostic or atheistic principles, the government's protection of its citizens' freedoms of religion, speech, assembly, and family integrity requires that it not abrogate responsibilities originally and properly belonging to homes and schools. When government fulfills its own responsibilities in this fashion, it thereby helps strengthen the common commitment of all citizens to government.

The political/legal implications of this second approach are similar to those articulated in the previous chapter with regard to religion and the Republic. Recognition of parents' responsibility to choose schools for their children, when combined with the First Amendment's guarantee that religious freedom be protected, adds up to a different kind of legal authority for schooling. A wide variety of schools or school systems, each free on its own philosophical or religious basis to open its doors to students, should all be treated equitably by government.[5] This means that there should be proportionate public funding (whether by voucher or direct payment) of all schools—whether government-owned or not—so that all children receive equitable public support of their education.

Not only does such a system *not* violate the First Amendment; it is, from our point of view, the only system that can avoid violating the First Amendment. Any other system, including the one currently established, discriminates against those parents and schools who, for conscience sake, wish to educate children differently. Beginning in the nineteenth century, Catholics, for example, were unjustly treated by the Protestant majority. Today the discrimination is against anyone (atheist, Jew, Muslim, Christian, or secular humanist) who wishes to use a school other than government-run schools where the dominant ideology and pedagogy might be highly Protestant in some parts of the country, thoroughly secularistic in another part, or highly eclectic somewhere else.

As in the era when a single church was established under the conviction that a society could not hold together without such an establishment, today government-run schools have been established under the influence of an undifferentiated moral argument that our society cannot hold together without such a system. But acting on that assumption (with all of its legal consequences) in a culturally diverse society breeds the very dissension it intends to overcome. Insofar as citizens hold different views of education (just as they hold different ecclesiastical and theological views), the very act of giving public privilege to one school system turns schooling into a *political* battlefield where citizens must fight for government control. Not only is schooling thereby jeopardized; political order itself is threatened by the competition for control over one of its central institutions—the school. Moral arguments over what constitutes good schooling—arguments that ought to occur in the arena of educational-moral debate—become politicized because of an undifferentiated moral conviction that education itself belongs to the original competence of government. In the American political arena as now constituted that kind of moral starting point requires that the winner take all and that a single, majoritarian consensus should be established by government in the public arena.

The Differentiation of State and School

If, however, a different set of assumptions were to take hold and government were to be seen as a civic authority over citizens who are recognized as legitimately diverse in their religions, educational ideals, family traditions, and so forth, then a common set of *civic* requirements could be designed in concert with the full protection of a diverse system of schools freely chosen by families. What is required is that we shift from undifferentiated to differentiated moral reasoning. If, politically speaking, American citizens can agree to disagree about schooling, just as they have agreed in constitutional law to disagree about theology and church life, then the framework of actual *political and legal agreement* can become stronger. If we can *agree* that the legal mandate for all citizens should be that each gets a tax-supported education *and* that the contexts of that education may *legitimately* be as diverse as the American people want them to be, then we can flourish as families and educators in our diverse modes of moral reasoning about schooling while *as citizens* we conduct a different kind of public-moral argument about what justice demands for the fair treatment of all schools.

The gist of this argument is to urge American citizens to replace the current political/educational establishment with something better. Just as the founders disestablished the church in order to establish ecclesiastical pluralism, so today we should disestablish the state-monopoly school system and establish a tax-supported pluralistic school system. This argument is not first of all about education but about just governance. The point is that we need not try to achieve *political* agreement about what constitutes good education. We need only agree that a just political order necessitates respect for family integrity, for diverse schools, and for the education of all citizens, and that apart from such respect justice cannot be done to citizens.

If this morally differentiated, *public-legal* argument can be won, then, as a consequence, we as citizens will no longer have to keep arguing and fighting *politically* to define the internal contents of schooling for all students. Disputes over curricular and educational philosophy will thereby be removed from the arena of political conflict and debate and left in the hands of educators and parents in a diverse array of settings—each enjoying the same degree of public funding and support. As citizens who hold in common the political and legal order, however, we will then be able to concentrate on legislative and judicial matters that concern the commons that we all share.

Part of what we will hold in common *as citizens* will be a new pluralistic school system that each of us can treasure because it does justice to all. Children will no longer be viewed as people who have to undergo schooling designed by the majority before they are allowed to gain entrance to public life. A public agreement to legalize educational pluralism will be parallel to civic agreements we have already reached, namely, that citizens do not first of all have to own property before they can vote; that they do not first have to become Congregationalists or Episcopalians before they may enjoy the full rights of citizenship; and that they do not first have to be white or male in order to become first-class citizens.

A political agreement to pluralize and disestablish education is not a shallow device for avoiding controversy. It is a means of justly distinguishing—differentiating—spheres of life and discourse that really are different. To fail to differentiate church from state, or school from state, or family from state leads inevitably to confusion in moral discourse when people try to argue for what *ought* to be done. A moral argument requires clarification of who is responsible to do what. Insofar as there are real differences of responsibility in different areas of life, it is incumbent upon us to become morally differentiated in our discourse and decision-making.

As educators and parents we can and must continue our moral debates over what is good pedagogy and child care, over what is the best training for children at different stages of social, intellectual, and moral development. As people with ecclesiastical and theological responsibilities, we should continue our debates with one another over the truth about God and human nature. But it is essential for responsible civic discourse that *as citizens* we focus debate on political truth and error, not on areas of life that are not government's responsibility. As citizens we should no longer make pedagogy or theology the responsibility of government such that we then must fight political battles to decide what is correct education or correct theology. What we should do as citizens is to work toward agreements about how government ought to do justice to those who also happen to be theologically and ecclesiastically diverse believers and educationally diverse family members and educators. A just state in other words, according to our political-moral argument, is one that both recognizes the responsibilities of nonpolitical spheres of life and also treats the diverse expressions in each of those spheres with proportionate equity. Individuals, families, and schools must no longer be reduced to functions of the Republic conceived of as a morally undifferentiated community.

Our moral argument obviously calls into question the authority of the civic republican tradition, which sees schooling as belonging to the original competence of the state—a state supposedly directed by the single will of its majority. We challenge the idea that for a polity to be unified its citizens (or at least the majority of them) have to be catechized into the same view of life in a common school.

It is this undifferentiated confounding of schooling and governing that aggravates the current debate over multiculturalism and keeps it from a resolution. Arthur Schlesinger, who is on one side of the multicultural debate, opposes many of today's multiculturalists for trying to force upon public schooling a curricular agenda that would deny the possibility of common cultural ideals and a common interpretation of history. However, he and other traditional liberals continue to depend upon the political process in order to hold onto an older view that was established in public schools. Schlesinger believes that the older view of a common American history, taught in common schools, can do justice to society's ethnic and cultural diversity. Schlesinger as well as his multicultural opponents are, in fact, agreeing to fight an all-or-nothing political battle for winner-take-all stakes over the terrain of public education. Consequently, the particular merits of their different views of history cannot come into full view or receive fair treatment because of the unnecessary (and, from our point of view, illegitimate) politicization of education that escapes their notice but dictates the terms of the debate.

Schlesinger believes that cultural pluralism and the teaching of Afro-American history, for example, are legitimate, but what he objects to is "the teaching of *bad* history under whatever ethnic banner."[6] But who is supposed to decide what is good or bad history? Without differentiating his moral argument for good history from his moral argument for a unified polity, Schlesinger accepts the political terms of battle as appropriate for the settling of an academic question. Schlesinger sees the "Afrocentric campaign"[7] in New York State, for example, as having the aim of turning education (including history teaching) into a "therapeutic" tool. "Race consciousness and group pride are supposed to strengthen a sense of identity and self-respect among nonwhite students."[8] Schlesinger objects to this ideal of education because it is an outgrowth of a form of nationalism that he finds culturally reductionistic and confining. There is a "certain inauthenticity," says Schlesinger,

> in saddling public schools with the mission of convincing children of the beauties of their particular ethnic origins. The ethnic subcultures, if they had genuine vitality, would be sufficiently instilled in children by family, church and community. It is surely not the office of the public school to promote artificial ethnic chauvinism.[9]

"When every ethnic and religious group claims a right to approve or veto anything that is taught in public schools, the fatal line is crossed between cultural pluralism and ethnocentrism."[10] What is that "fatal line," in Schlesinger's opinion? It is the loss of "the old idea that whatever our ethnic base, we are all Americans together."[11]

Clearly, Schlesinger is unable to recognize his own political-moral prejudice for what it is. He opposes "nationalism" of a particular ethnonationalist version. But he holds close to his heart his own liberal version of nationalism—the story of an American nation whose unity transcends (and is capable of incorporating) all ethnic, religious, and other diversities. Only this view of the nation deserves to be taught in government-established schools. The teaching of all other nationalist tales can be done quite adequately in the privacy of homes, churches, and parochial communities; only the truly nonsectarian tale about all of us being "Americans together" should be taught in the public schools.

The question, of course, is whether this idea of truth, namely, Schlesinger's liberal interpretation of national unity, ought to be forced on citizens through a government-controlled school system when some American citizens hold a different view of truth in general and of the nation's history in particular. Schlesinger seems not to remember that the kind of national educational unity he now supports was itself organized and politicized in the nineteenth century for therapeutic reasons by the cultural majority. The Protestant majority said that Catholics and others were free to instill ethnic and religious pride in their children at home, in their churches, and in their ethnic communities, but the purpose of public schooling should be to produce common citizens who would share a common pride in being Americans—the latter being defined, of course, by the WASP majority. Schlesinger does not want schools to teach an artificial ethnic chauvinism but to instill the truth about a common history. But who decides what is "artificial"? The WASP idea of a "common America" seemed pretty artificial to many American immigrants in the nineteenth century. In the present system, whoever controls the schools politically will decide the matter of authenticity and artificiality. But will a majoritarian political victory, whether by the Schlesingers or by the multicultural opposition, be able to determine academic authenticity and truth?

James Hunter does a better job than Schlesinger of describing the polarized culture war over American schooling. But he also seems to interpret that conflict as one that will be resolved only by one side winning victory.[12] Hunter is not ready to propose a pluralist school system made possible by means of a moral differentiation between schooling and governing.

In place of these undifferentiated moralisms, which require the fighting of all-or-nothing political battles throughout much of American social life, we offer the proposition that the political/legal order is a specifically differentiated commons to be shaped in accord with the standard of just treatment for all citizens. Why not give equal treatment to the variety of religions and cultural worldviews as they express themselves in public life and in various nongovernmental institutions such as families, schools, and churches? Let the moral battles over the truth of history, theology, science, and philosophy be fought in an open cultural arena without political prejudice. What ought to bind the polity together, we believe, is not an extrapolitical or extralegal glue such as a common church, or cultural homogeneity, or racial uniformity, or a politically cobbled school curriculum. In fact, every political attempt to build the civic commons on the basis of forced conformity to a religious creed, racial designation, political ideology, or schooling pattern (even if it meets with the approval of the majority) seems to produce the fruits of its own dissolution. A common polity is a sharing in a common legal/political order. That polity maintains the support of citizens insofar as they are convinced that its laws treat them all fairly. It does not require the political imposition of a common educational or political ideology. It requires the just treatment of personal and social diversity.

Conclusion

Current American laws governing schooling are, in fact, a mixture of the two traditions contrasted above. On the one hand, the dominant tradition is that of Jefferson, Mann, and Dewey—now codified in state-run systems of common schools that own the privilege of public funding and government backing of their curricular offerings. This tradition requires political decision-making (and thus political/legal "warfare") over every significant curricular reform.

On the other hand, current law also recognizes the parental right of opting out of the public system at private expense. It grants some degree of private freedom for nongovernment schools, including religious schools, if they pay their own way. So the Jeffersonian conviction that every child should receive a free education in a common school has never been universally enforced. Furthermore, in deference to the First Amendment's religious-freedom guarantee, an accommodation has been made at various points in recent decades to grant some public funding to children who go to nongovernment schools. In fact, part of the conflict among American citizens now—part of our culture war—is over the inherent ambiguity of this current legal framework. Many citizens want a more consistent Jeffersonian establishment—a common school coupled with the complete prohibition of all public funding for nongovernment schools. Others, however, want a consistent pluralism that respects the prior authority of parents in the rearing of their children and freedom to choose schools without financial or legal discrimination.[13]

Would not the move to genuine educational pluralism, we ask, lead to both a fairer treatment of diverse families and schools—the *pluribus*—and a greater commitment from Americans to the *unum* of the public commons we all share? Once citizens recognize that they are all being treated fairly and that parents' freedom to educate their children does not depend on the ability to win majority political power, then all citizens would have a new reason for wanting to support the common law that promotes educational opportunity for every citizen in ways that comport with the integrity of each home, school, faith, and culture.

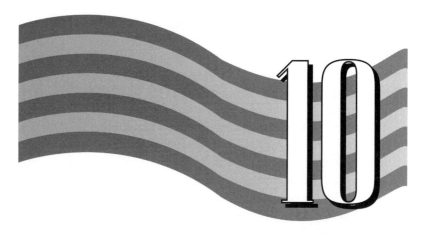

Public Discourse and Electoral Representation

A polity—a political community—has its own identity distinct from the families, schools, churches, enterprises, and many other organizations that function within its territory and under its public law. Citizens under government constitute a political order with its own distinct responsibilities. This is the arena in which people are bound together in a commonwealth, a political *unum,* sharing common civic rights and responsibilities. If, as we argued in the previous two chapters, it is necessary to distinguish between the moral discourse appropriate to a church from that which is appropriate to politics, between that which pertains to schooling from that which pertains to doing public justice, then how should citizens, *as citizens,* best be organized for the conduct of political-moral argument?

The main tradition of American politics takes for granted that the Republic is, or ought to be, a community of free and rational individuals who share what Jefferson called a common moral sense as guide to the shaping of the public good. Our Constitution establishes a federal government and presupposes state governments that are to serve the people as citizens. These checked and balanced governments are not supposed to fall prey to unrestrained majorities, to usurpatious minorities, or to any single interest group. The Constitution is, furthermore, the guarantor of a variety of individual rights over against government.

The system of electoral representation that has been established within this framework is one designed to facilitate the realization of civic consensus (made manifest through a single, majority will) amid multiple and competing interests. Citizens are supposed to conduct debate during electoral contests in which the selection of representatives will set the direction for future policy making. Campaign debates culminate in voting—a process carried out in single-member electoral districts where, by majority vote, one candidate will be chosen to represent everyone in the district. A majority (or plurality) vote wins; the winner takes all. Those who vote against the winner (the minority, or plural minorities) are not thought to be unrepresented after the election but rather are considered to be represented by the winner, who, by definition, represents the will of the whole.

In this electoral system, minorities are not expected to be represented independently but are to have protection in their persons and properties from an overreaching majority. Minority political opinions deserve the same protection that other parochial opinions deserve, namely, the right to free expression outside the majority governing process. Political debate during election times, therefore, is a debate oriented toward winning a majority vote in order to identify those who will be authorized to enter legislative and executive offices to govern.

But now, this question: What if U.S. citizens do not, in fact, constitute a homogeneous political mass? What if their political views cannot adequately be condensed into a single, majority viewpoint, especially when electoral majorities appear to be increasingly thin and artificial? The United States is, to be sure, a single republic, but what if citizens differ significantly in their views of the Republic, as happens to be the case with libertarians, nationalists, utilitarians, pragmatists, socialists, liberal egalitarians, conservative republicans, and Christian-democratic pluralists? In that case, does it make sense to have an electoral system that forces citizens to seek an unrepresentative, majoritarian, electoral conclusion?

If one's view of political life and one's concern for a sound program of government is grounded in a morally coherent worldview different from the views of other citizens, how can one feel satisfied with an electoral process that frustrates the desire to engage in serious public-moral debate from that point of view? What should people do if political debate is inhibited or shunted aside by an electoral process structured as a simple horse race and by a legislative process that has increasingly become one of interest-group brokering?

Could it be that the American electoral process has become as ill-suited to a culturally and religiously diverse society as the current public school system is ill-suited to that same society? Is there not a better way to structure the electoral process to make serious public debate possible among our diverse citizenry? Serious debate about the political *unum* will become possible, we believe, only if the electoral system allows genuinely competitive debate to occur among the actual diversity of citizens and quits forcing them into artificial, bipolar camps in the struggle to gain winner-take-all majority power.

Assessing the Problems

Because of an unhealthy takeover by media, money, and marketing, says W. Lance Bennett, Americans now find themselves being manipulated by an electoral system that no longer provides for meaningful representation. We have entered an era "in which electoral choices are of little consequence because an electoral system in disarray can generate neither the party unity nor the levels of public agreement necessary to forge a winning and effective political coalition."[1]

The goal of our Republic, argues George Will, should be "deliberative democracy through representatives who function at a constitutional distance from the people."[2] Today, however, we no longer have "an ethic, or a political philosophy, or a constitutional doctrine that encourages people to distinguish between licit and illicit advantages from government."[3] To the contrary, "the problem is the everydayness of, the routinization of, the banality of the process by which private interests methodically seek to bend public power to private purposes."[4]

These statements, along with dozens of others that could be added, point to a problem of complex proportions. The evidence suggests that numerous interconnected aspects of our political system are implicated in a diffuse crisis. It is not merely campaign-finance laws, or interest-group pressures, or career incumbency that can be singled out as the sole culprit. These along with many other aspects of our electoral and governance systems appear to be linked together in an intricate web of declining civic faith, electoral apathy or antipathy, and governmental disorder.

There appears to be an intensifying incongruity between our expanding, highly mobile, multicultural population, on the one hand, and the means by which that population is formally represented in Washington, on the other. There is an expanding gap between the decreasing significance of national elections and the growing power of unrepresentative interest groups and of "rights talk." The need for Congress and the president to act responsibly on behalf of the country as a whole is thwarted by a system that allows less and less room for public deliberation about the common good, about the broad national interest. The recovery of deliberative democracy, of confidence in government, and of meaningful representation can take place, it would seem, only if Americans can make changes that will systematically and simultaneously alter many aspects of the political system.

There are at least six components of our democratic system that now appear to be aggravating one another in a downward spiral that threatens to undermine the governance of the country.

1. Our huge country of more than 250 million people has only a *single* elected official—the president—to represent everyone. Even though the Congress as a whole is co-responsible for federal governance, no senator or representative is elected with a responsibility to serve the common good of the country as a whole.

James L. Sundquist, a senior fellow emeritus of The Brookings Institution, explains that since all members of Congress are elected by districts, "Congress *as a whole* is not accountable to the people *as a whole*. Each voter can act to throw out one rascal, but the others are beyond reach. . . . Thus the Congress is in a very real sense an irresponsible body, beyond control by the voters, whatever their mood."[5]

2. National political parties, which function primarily in connection with presidential campaigns, are almost powerless to mold national agendas that can bind elected officials together in their respective parties for governance after an election. The party structures that exist perform a very small percentage of the work necessary for meaningful representation in a modern democracy. Today's political par-

ties, says Will, are "mere money-raising and money-distributing oper-
ations, and not even the most important raisers and disbursers."[6]

> Running for Congress is today an activity akin to pure entrepreneur-
> ship on the part of candidates who put themselves forward. They find
> a market (a district) and a market niche (a potential majority to be cob-
> bled together from various factions); they merchandise themselves with
> advertising paid for by venture capitalists (contributors) who invest in
> candidates.[7]

Our political parties as they now function are unable to hold elected
party members accountable to govern as disciplined teams in accord
with campaign platforms and promises.[8]

3. Individuals who win elections in our system each represent a voting *district* rather than a constituency that belongs to the same party
as the winning candidate. What this means is that as many as half the
voters (along with many who do not vote) end up being "represented"
by individuals they wish were *not* representing them. That is to say,
many voters have as their official representative the candidate they
actually voted against. This is because our electoral system is structured by single-member districts, in each of which a winner "takes
all." Thus, the already weak link between most citizens and their elected
officials is further weakened by the decidedly antipathetic attitude of
some citizens toward members of Congress. Moreover, evidence suggests that this antipathy is easily transferred to government as a whole
and is not confined to particular representatives.[9]

4. Most voters have so little positive connection with those who
supposedly represent them that they feel alienated from (and often
antipathetic toward) the political process generally. In fact, in federal
elections over the past few decades, close to 50 percent of the eligible
voters have not bothered to vote. And even among those who have
voted, most know little or nothing about the officeholder who represents the district in which they live. "Most Americans today," says
Bennett, "experience elections as empty rituals that offer little hope
for political dialogue, genuine glimpses of candidate character, or the
emergence of a binding consensus on where the nation is going and
how it ought to get there."[10]

5. Elected representatives, identified with political parties that are
too weak to hold them accountable and representing districts where
half or more of the voters are apathetic or antipathetic, are officials

who function essentially as lone rangers.[11] This is true both in the running of their campaigns as well as in the way they serve in elected office. This makes concerted congressional action on behalf of the public even more difficult to achieve. Elected representatives who are neither tied together by party discipline nor obligated by election mandates find that they must deal with other demands and pressures that are more forceful and direct, namely, the demands from organized interest groups.

6. The most influential political connections that the president and most senators and representatives have today are in fact with interest groups, not with national parties or supporting voters in their districts. This holds true both for the conduct of business in their elected offices as well as for the conduct of election campaigns and the fund-raising necessary for those campaigns. Will says that governments have always responded to interests, but today the word "respond" is far too benign to capture the truth about political reality. "The modern state does not merely respond to interests, it generates them and even, in effect, organizes them."[12]

Considering together these six interconnected components of the federal election and governing systems, we can take note of at least two very profound and dire consequences. The first is that elected representatives now function chiefly as interest-group brokers rather than as public-interest representatives or trustees of the national commonwealth. This is the judgment that Bennett reaches in developing his criticism of campaign finance laws, of the marketing of candidates, and of the distorting connection between contemporary politics and the media. Individual candidates at all levels, he says, "have been separated from their party loyalties by an elaborate system of individual funding from interest groups. . . . There is precious little room left for thinking about—much less, acting on—any broader public interest."[13]

> Celluloid candidates and imaginary issues are just the symptoms of deeper problems with the system. The weakening link between elections and governing is the more fundamental problem. . . . [T]he centrifugal pull of special interests at every level of government has left little chance for coherent action on pressing public problems. Simply enacting a national budget each year has become a major challenge and frequent crisis of governing.[14]

The second consequence is that most citizens who do choose to engage in civic action at the national level now put most of their time and money into the interest-group pressuring game, or they take off into protest movements, marches, and litigation in the courts. Less and less civic action materializes in the form of mature, public-interest debate during and after election campaigns among competing parties offering alternative, substantive programs. The truth is that citizens *are* relatively powerless either to give clear mandates at election time or to hold individual representatives accountable once they enter office. Interest-group activism—beyond control of the political parties and of Congress—appears to most citizens to be the primary means of exercising political influence even though it is a means that almost never allows for a consideration of the law-making process from a public-interest viewpoint—that is, from a point of view concerned with the commonwealth as a whole, with the common good of the entire Republic.

Interest-group politics in turn increasingly squeezes Congress into the mold of an interest-group brokerage house, so that the Republic is left without representative governance in the original and full sense of that term. As Bennett puts it:

> The fragmentation of the governing system has at once produced a decline in broad, programmatic national policies and an increase of what might be called government in the trenches. Both on Capitol Hill and in the executive branch, committee and agency personnel are working overtime writing the rules and regulations that bring thousands of small fragmentary policies on line consistent with the interests of the groups that have pushed them into legislative and bureaucratic agendas. This flurry of micro politics belies any suggestion that government has ceased activity. Rather, government has become even more dedicated to the writing and rewriting of rules and regulations and haggling over where federal responsibilities lie for increasingly uncoordinated politics. The point is simply that government is less and less occupied with passing laws backed by the force of governing ideas.[15]

In sum, our predicament is this: Americans—*as citizens*—no longer seem to be represented in a way that allows them to fulfill their public-interest responsibilities; parties are too weak to connect voters to those who win elections; and interest-group brokering has displaced public-interest statecrafting to the point where more and more citizens realize that the Republic does not have an accountable government in Washington.

What Representation Should Mean

Before turning to recommendations for reform that might begin to address this complex network of problems, we must first ask what representative government should mean. Surely one of the first principles of a sound electoral system is that it should serve to galvanize strong connections between citizens and their elected representatives. That is what democracy is supposed to be all about. It seems doubtful to us, however, that these connections can be restored simply by means of "term limits" as advocated by George Will. Term limits focus almost exclusively on the dispositions and actions of individual representatives and senators rather than on the organizational accountability of political parties and of Congress as a whole. Will's hope of restoring deliberative democracy hangs entirely on the idea of replacing "professional careerists" with ordinary citizens who will not be able to grow attached to public office.[16]

For Will's argument to succeed term limits would have to do more than simply cut short legislative careers. Term limits would have to reinstate something like an eighteenth-century world of greater cultural homogeneity in which geographically settled citizens would find it possible to trust their amateur politicians (sent to Washington from single-member districts) to deliberate thoroughly and arrive at sound policies that advance the national interest. The mere fact of *not* being able to have a career in elected office would have to be powerful enough to induce the kind of deliberation that produces common insight into the national interest, even though each representative and senator would still be elected to represent only one district and not the country as a whole. Will treats the problems of contemporary representation as if political parties are superfluous and as if voters require no additional means to hold Congress and the president accountable.[17]

Our view of what it will take to reconnect citizens positively with their elected representatives in Washington is quite different from Will's. Something more significant than merely cutting short the incumbency of careerists is necessary, especially when some of those careerists happen to be the best public servants in the country. Elected representatives acting deliberately—even those whose ambition it is to work for the common good on the basis of the strongest possible civic faith— do not, *individually*, make national policy. Congress as a body determines the shape of legislation. The question, then, is not first of all about the disposition of individuals in office but about the conditions and forces that shape the teamwork that produces healthy or unhealthy policy outcomes.

We believe that in a healthy democracy political parties should be stronger than interest groups since the latter neither submit to elections nor come under widespread popular control. Parties, through which citizens organize themselves *as citizens* for elections and for governance, should have greater power in shaping national policy than do the groups that intentionally lobby for particular interests and not for the common good. Political parties should function as serious team builders, closely connecting the citizens who are their members with candidates for the Senate, the House, and the presidency so that candidates no longer run as free-wheeling individuals and are no longer left to function chiefly as interest-group brokers once in office. Political parties should function as potent, public accountability structures, doing more than simply coordinating minor campaign tasks for lone-ranger candidates who remain dependent on extraparty PAC contributions. Parties should have to bear the burden of responsibility for devising full platforms and programs with which to guide and discipline their candidates—platforms and programs that can be put to the test of public judgment in elections. Citizens, in other words, need to be able to hold candidates accountable as members of party teams both before and after elections.

Furthermore, in a highly mobile, multicultural, and ideologically diverse society a sound electoral system ought to make possible the representation of actual citizens rather than the representation of artificial and often absurdly gerrymandered voting districts. All voters, not simply the winning majorities in separate districts, should be able to see and feel the direct connection between their votes and those who represent them in Washington. The electoral system should be structured to invite rather than discourage voter participation. All voters should have the opportunity to get involved in the kind of civic debate and campaigning that can make a real difference at election time.

A workable system of representation, from our point of view, should also generate a greater number of national political leaders—members of the House and Senate who are recognized by people across the country as representing their point of view and their program goals for government. Civic debate that has real political significance should occur during electoral contests among national party leaders who represent party teams. These leaders, moreover, need to be accountable primarily to citizens through their parties rather than to interest groups.

In sum, American citizens should have an electoral system that allows all of them to be represented meaningfully, that encourages the growth of strong parties that connect voters and elected officials closely, and that elevates public-interest statecrafting above interest-group brokering as the chief task of government in Washington.

How Do We Get a System That Will Work?

Reforming the American electoral system in order to strengthen genuine representation and to make that representation a tool of public-interest government requires a means of connecting voters directly and powerfully with their official representatives—a connection that is politically stronger than either the link between voters and interest groups or the link between representatives and interest groups. The electoral system devised by most democracies in the world to serve this purpose is one that allows almost every vote to count, not just those of the majority, and one that puts the burden of governance on citizen-connected parties rather than on freewheeling interest-group brokers. It is called proportional representation, or PR for short.[18]

While there are many ways to design an electoral system with greater or lesser degrees of proportional representation (PR), we suggest a first step that simply alters the method of electing members to our House of Representatives while leaving everything else about the Senate, the presidency, and the federal system intact.[19] Once this first step is taken, however, even if only in a few states, we believe the consequences can gradually unfold constructively to touch each of the problems outlined above.[20]

Under current law, population determines the number of seats allotted to each state in the House of Representatives. For the entire country a numerical proportion is calculated between the number of House seats (435) and the total U.S. population. Each seat is supposed to represent the same number of people. Once that number is determined, each state knows how many representatives it may have based on its population. Each state then carves up its territory into the number of districts corresponding to the number of House seats it may fill. Each of those districts then becomes a single-member election zone to be represented in Congress by the candidate who wins a majority (or plurality) of the votes cast in the election. It is easy to see that the election winner represents a voting *district*, which includes more than the citizens who vote for the winning candidate. Those who voted for the losing candidate (or candidates) in that district will also be "represented" by the winner. All the losing votes—even if they add up to 49 percent or more of the ballots cast—achieve nothing. In simple terms, ours is a winner-take-all system.

This is the root cause of the lack of electoral competitiveness in our system. On the surface there appears to be fierce competition between candidates, and each year more and more money is spent on campaigns. But underneath the personality contests we do not often find significantly contrasting program alternatives from which to choose. Our system tends to eliminate all but two candidates in any district, and each of them battles just to get 51 percent of the vote in order to win everything. Each wants to appeal to as many voters as possible and to alienate as few as possible. Strong, detailed, and specific contrasts disappear. The strongest competition between candidates is for campaign contributions with which to pay for superficial TV and other media advertisements.[21] Candidates who can appeal to only a minority of the population tend to be squeezed out of electoral contests.[22] Voter apathy and antipathy spring from the growing incongruity between the appearance that something significant is happening and the deeper reality that the election campaign's outcome is likely to be inconsequential.

In place of this winner-take-all system of individualized, expensive, and superficial contests in single-member districts, we propose that each state be turned into a *single, multimember* district from which its allotted number of House seats would be filled by a means of PR (proportional representation). For example, if Illinois is allowed twenty-two seats in the House of Representatives, our proposed reform would permit any number of political parties each to run twenty-two candidates for the entire state in an election that would determine the winners by a proportional count. If the Democrats were to win 50 percent of the vote across the State, they would get eleven seats in the House, not more or less. If the Republicans were to win 35 percent of the vote, they would get eight seats in the House, not more or less. If the Green Party, the Libertarian Party, and the Rainbow Coalition were each to win 5 percent of the vote, then each would get one seat in the House, not more or less.

Not only would nearly every vote count in this PR system—with minority as well as majority parties gaining representation—but nearly every voter would be represented in the House by the party he or she actually votes for. All who vote Democrat, no matter where they live in the state, would be represented by the Democrat team. All who vote Republican would be represented by the Republican team. All who vote Green or Libertarian (or some other) would be represented by the party they actually vote for—if that party wins at least 5 percent of the vote.

Here is the beginning of a real *connection*—of genuine account-ability—between voters as citizens and the official representatives they elect. It also opens the way to other benefits. For example, PR allows groups of citizens, even small groups, to gain representation through the electoral process without in any way inhibiting a genuine major-ity—even a very large majority—from winning control of the House. Instead of citizens giving up at the start because they feel their votes will not count (since under the current system those votes often do not count), they will instead be motivated under PR to work together to organize parties that can try to win a percentage of the House seats at election time. They will not have to win a majority of votes in a sin-gle district in order to assure themselves of representation. They will, however, have to work together to develop meaningful principles and programs sufficient to bind a sizable group of citizens together.

Criticisms of Proportional Representation

An argument for proportional representation faces at least two crit-icisms. The first is that too many parties might come into existence and thus cause governmental instability if no party is able to gain majority control of the House. The second criticism is that a statewide slate of party representatives would not guarantee voters a personal representative close to home—from the particular district where they live. Let us consider each of these criticisms.

In the first place, a greater number of parties may be precisely what the country needs if the diversity of its citizens is greater than can be represented by a superficial majority in a two-party system. Would it not be better, in other words, for everyone to see in Congress exactly how diverse the body politic is than to be misled by the impression that the Democrats and Republicans adequately represent the entire body politic? More parties in a system that allows for better and truer representation might bring greater rather than less stability to our system because it would make for greater voter confidence in elected representatives. The real question is whether the *present* system is any longer stable.

Second, we must be careful not to compare apples with oranges as if they are the same fruit. A system of PR tends, as we will argue below, to create parties that are more disciplined and coherent, each with a definite program and philosophy. Even if six or eight parties gained significant representation in the House, and even if none of them held a majority of seats, the process of negotiation and accommodation among them would likely be less chaotic and more purposeful than under the current system. Why? At present, majority control of the House by the Democrats gives a superficial impression of coherent, one-party control. But in many respects, given the nature of our undisciplined parties and the interest-group influence on individual committees and representatives, the process of negotiation typically involves far more than six or eight groups or camps. When the dominant party has no binding program to discipline all of its members, and when each member is tied significantly to unofficial interest groups, far more chaos, gridlock, and incoherence are likely to be evident among 435 negotiators and compromisers than would be the case if only six or eight well-defined and disciplined parties were negotiating over a bill.

In the third place, most countries that employ a system of PR typically fix as a threshold a certain percentage of votes that any party must win in order to gain representation. In other words, there is a relatively simple way to avoid the problem of subjecting the House to the onslaught of too many small parties. A typical threshold, for example, is 5 percent; a party, in other words, would have to win at least 5 percent of the vote in order to gain a seat from any state.[23]

Establishing a threshold like this would clearly inhibit the proliferation of parties. For governing purposes this can be justified, though it does compromise the principle that every voter should have the right to be represented by a party of conviction. Our proposal already compromises the principle of pure PR regardless of whether a threshold is established. In proposing to keep the state boundaries intact, our proposal recognizes that states with heavy population concentrations—such as New York and California—will have far greater potential for genuine PR than will states such as Montana and the Dakotas. A pure system of PR for the House would turn the entire country into a single, multimember district in which any number of parties could each run 435 candidates.

Fourth and finally, it is important to point out that evidence gathered over time from the experience of other democracies (most of which have some system of proportional representation) shows that PR by itself is not the cause of government instability.[24] Instability of government typically has more to do with the governing system than it does with the electoral system. We are not proposing to change the three-branch system of American federal government to a parliamentary system in which the executive is determined by the winning party or by a coalition of parties in the parliament. As long as our president is elected independently to head the government, then PR in the House will never leave the United States without a government.

As for the second criticism that PR denies citizens a personal and local representative in Washington, we must look carefully at what would be lost and gained in the change to a new system. Part of our criticism of the present system of single-member districts is that they have less and less meaning as actual localities of public, civic identity. Gerrymandered districts often take on such strange shapes that they mean nothing to the people who live in them apart from functioning to secure a winner-take-all personality who is available in Washington to perform "constituency services."[25] The present system has drained away much of the original meaning of a "representative"—someone in whom fellow citizens place their confidence to make laws in the public interest. To the extent that a serious diminution of the representative's public legislative role has occurred (as exhibited in loss of voter confidence and actual distrust of government), it is a very weak argument that tries to defend the present system on the grounds that it provides citizens with a particular person to perform constituency services for them in Washington.

How much better it would be if citizens in a state could have *teams* of representatives—party teams—serving them in Washington. These would be legislators with whom voters could identify closely, sharing the same philosophy and legislative agenda. In other words, if the primary meaning of representation could be regained by way of a system that allows all voters to be connected closely to the House members of their chosen party, then often people would have *more* than one representative in the House from their state to serve them. PR allows citizens to select statewide party teams rather than only a single representative. Even more important, these statewide teams would combine with other statewide teams of the same party to form national party teams of similar conviction, principles, and program. It would finally become possible for citizens to gain the thing most lacking in our current system, namely, national parties that represent their convictions about, and perspectives on, the country as a whole.

It must also be said that there are electoral systems, such as the one currently operative in Germany, that combine elements of both proportional and district representation. Such a system might work well for House elections in the United States.[26] We are not proposing that here, however, because if PR for the House were to be introduced within the confines of present state borders and if the electoral system for Senate seats is left untouched, then ample recognition would be given to the most important traditional districts, namely, the states. The need now is to build strong national parties and at the same time to make it possible for a diverse citizenry to gain genuine representation through publicly significant elections. Debating the intricacies of more complex electoral systems, such as the one in Germany, would needlessly complicate matters at this stage.[27]

Movement Toward Greater Accountability in Washington

The core value of PR is to make genuine representation possible—to connect voters and elected officials together in an accountability structure that keeps attention focused on the public interest. Those who are elected by means of PR will be tied very closely to the citizens who are members of their party. No party is likely to put forward candidates at election time who do not come up through its ranks and stand for what the party stands for. Every candidate will be part of a team that continues to function after as well as before the election. The party will continue to shape and direct its principles, its programs, and its representatives. Since each candidate who gets elected will represent his or her party, each will continue to be closely watched, guarded, and disciplined by that party. In this kind of framework, career politicians can be a boon rather than a threat to good government.

This, rather than term limits, is the answer to the problem of the lack of accountability on the part of those whom Will denounces as careerists. Will's reasons for wanting to limit, by purely negative means, the number of terms that an individual can serve sound like little more than wishful thinking. Without changing anything else in the system; without seeking to strengthen parties; without looking for a way to allow all voters to be represented; without expecting any new kind of teamwork—without any of these needed reforms, Will pins his hopes on the illusion that by taking away some of the voters' last remaining responsibility, deliberative democracy can be restored.

> The object is to restore a healthier relationship between the citizen and the government. At bottom, the case for term limits rests on the belief that such limits will help Americans become reacquainted with the ideas and practices of republicanism as that idea was understood by the most reflective members of this Republic's founding generation. This requires restoring the status, and hence the competence, of Congress. Given the nature of modern government, such restoration requires breaking the dynamic of careerism. Term limits will break it. Limits are required to institutionalize healthy competition in the political market, just as antitrust intervention in economic markets can serve the values of a basically free market economy.[28]

Term limits might break the careerism of freewheeling individuals who are unconnected to parties and who therefore grow attached to interest groups. But what will break interest-group control of an even further individualized congressional membership? What meaningful competition will become possible if voters still have no opportunity to choose from among alternate governing programs put forward by parties that can discipline their elected representatives? Why will citizens, who currently feel alienated from politics, suddenly gain more interest in ancient republican ideas when they have not been given a single new or additional power by means of term limits?

The way to bring about accountable, deliberative government is to make it possible for citizens both to deliberate seriously (directly *as citizens* and not merely as members of interest groups) and to hold accountable the representatives they elect for the purpose of continuing that deliberation in Congress. The PR reform we are suggesting will help to do that by forcing a change in the way parties actually develop and function. Parties in a PR system have to work to define themselves very precisely and clearly in contrast to one another. Under PR, victory is gained not by candidates trying to be all things to all people and therefore saying as little as possible about what they will do in office. Rather, representation is gained by parties only in proportion to the number of votes won, and no party is able to "take all" by winning only 51 percent of the votes. Voters are free to vote for what they really believe in rather than simply for the lesser of evils. Under PR, voters gain the opportunity to learn more precisely what they are voting for, and if they do not like what they see in one party, they can vote for another party or work to start a new one. No party will be able to benefit from being fuzzy and noncommittal. Here we have the makings of real electoral competition.[29]

Furthermore, each party under the new system would be pushed to define what it plans to do on a wide range of concerns. It would, in other words, have to show why its program is best for the common good on a large number of issues. Some citizens, interested only in one issue, may of course try to organize a party around that single issue, but over time relatively few voters will cast their ballots for a party whose candidates refuse to address all the issues on which representatives are authorized to legislate in Congress. It will be too easy for another more comprehensive party to coopt that issue and thus to marginalize or eliminate single-issue parties. If interest groups want to exercise influence in the political arena, they will have to deal with citizens from the start, at the grass roots level where they are defining and organizing their parties; interest groups will no longer be able to buy up candidates individually before elections or wait until after the election to pressure representatives individually when they arrive in Washington. Citizens, in other words, would be able under PR to take charge of their representatives from start to finish and thereby deal with various interest-group pressures both prior to and following elections. Disciplined parties would have no reason to send lone rangers to Washington to become interest-group brokers outside party control.

This is the only fundamental way to get at current problems associated with campaign financing and interest-group control over candidates and representatives. All other measures will only be stopgaps. As long as citizens have no direct way to support the representatives in whom they wish to place their confidence they will feel powerless to hold accountable those who do win elections. Under those circumstances, nothing can be done to control interest groups that are able to forge a close connection between their members and their leaders.[30]

Only by putting real civic and electoral authority in the hands of citizens who are thereby able to hold representatives directly accountable will it be possible to subordinate private interest groups to the civic work of shaping law in the public interest for the common good.

Emergence of National Parties

Once the business of elections shifts from the buying and selling of individual candidates to campaign debates among disciplined parties with clearly articulated legislative agendas, voters will become more involved in learning to judge among different party programs. With respect to a national legislative agenda, each party will want to maximize its strength nationwide. Representatives from the Republican Party in Illinois, for example, will need to work closely with Republicans from other states. In fact, the initiative for organizing parties and party programs is most likely to gravitate to the national level.[31] Democrat, Republican, and other parties will organize nationally and begin to map out consistent and coherent strategies for their House campaigns in each state. Integral, comprehensive, and distinctive programs will be developed by each national party and then put before the electorate by the branches of that party in each state as the parties campaign under PR for House seats. Any party that can demonstrate nationwide coherence and strength will have an advantage over parties that cannot demonstrate such capabilities.

One consequence of the emergence of national parties is that a greater number of national leaders will also begin to appear. Each party will, in essence, put forward its best people for election. The most outstanding leaders of each party will, of course, have to win election in particular states. If one of the leaders of the Democrats happens to reside in Illinois, he or she will be able to enter Congress only by winning a seat in that state. But clearly that leader and others who win Democrat seats across the country will become national leaders representing everyone who is a member of, or who votes for, the Democrats.

Additional consequences that are likely to follow from the formation of national parties and from the rise of national political leaders will include a more thorough apprenticeship for future candidates, the recruitment of a greater number of statecrafters into parties with comprehensive agendas, and a deepening of experience on the part of ordinary citizens who learn to practice real political teamwork over time. Under the new system, parties will have a tough time surviving if they limit themselves to raising money at election time for empty and meaningless campaigns of a few individuals who have loosely chosen that party's label for themselves. Instead, parties will have to begin doing the remaining 90 percent of the hard work that mature political parties must do, namely, educate and recruit members; train and keep close tabs on leaders; develop serious platforms and programs; do policy research; work as teams to clarify the distinctive contributions of their party's program in contrast to other party programs; and conduct ongoing coalition efforts with other parties where ideas and programs overlap or coincide.

Conclusion

Under the new system proposed here we would, in all probability, witness the rise of a variety of strong national parties serving to represent nearly every voter (and not just voting districts) in Congress. A greater number of national leaders, working with party teams, would give all citizens a voice in political debate. Interest-group politics could gradually be demoted to second place behind genuine party politics. And citizens could begin to experience real and direct representation in a more deliberative Congress. In all probability voter turnout would increase, and the demand for statecrafting could grow in strength as interparty negotiations and accommodations begin to displace interest-group brokering in Congress. By means of such a system, the unity of the political order is reconciled with the true diversity of the citizenry. The pluralism of political convictions is respected and channeled through real competition into shared responsibility for the political order—the commonwealth that belongs to all citizens.

In Defense of Justice for All

The foregoing argument for a just political and legal order—an order defined in part by the principles of structural and confessional pluralism for a differentiated society—is an explicit moral argument self-conscious about its roots in the Christian faith. It does not pretend to be neutral. To affirm as we have done the merits of an open society in which all citizens are treated with equal respect under the law is to make a particular kind of public-moral argument. The proposals we have made for greater pluralism of religious expression, education, and political representation may sound too radical to some people. But these suggestions for reform arise from the conviction that the critical condition of American law and politics is tied very directly to long-standing patterns of injustice fueled by mistaken ideas about religion and what should constitute a political community. The public crisis (or crises) will not be resolved, we believe, without changes that recognize more clearly the differentiated moral responsibilities (including political responsibilities) of America's culturally diverse society. It is entirely fitting, then, that we should conclude with a brief summary of our basic presuppositions about human nature, creation order, historical development, societal differentiation, and public justice rooted, as we believe they are, in biblical revelation.

The Biblical Tradition

The widest, most encompassing context of human life, from the standpoint of biblical revelation, is the kingdom of God—that is, the rule of God over the entire creation. Everything that exists, in all of its diversity, has its identity as part of God's one creation. God governs the entire cosmos as Creator, Judge, and Redeemer. The creation is a wonderfully diversified unity. Human political order plays a limited and subordinate role under God in the larger scheme of things. Even the historical polity of ancient Israel—God's chosen people—became disposable when God enforced the covenant's sanctions in judgment against Israel's sin. And in the process God reaffirmed through the prophets the universal scope of divine authority.

From a biblical point of view, both the historical differentiation of society and the pervasively religious character of human life are inherent in the creation's meaningful dependence on the Creator. If God's authority encompasses the entire creation, and if human beings, along with every other creature, have their meaning in this context, then obviously all of life is religiously tied to God, and no single institution or community on earth can function as the all-encompassing master or integrator of human society. If the fullest *unum* of life is God's integral and all-embracing creation, then every differentiated institution or community of human existence must be seen as part of the diversity (the *pluribus*) in that larger unity. In that case, any particular political *unum* is itself never more than a limited part of the diversity of God's creation. The unifying character of a political order has to be of a limited kind—in this case of a differentiated, public-legal nature.

The historical clarification of this truth began at the beginning of Israel's independence—in the exodus from Egypt. The God of the covenant displayed supremacy over the supposedly omnicompetent kingdom of the pharaohs. Egypt, like many other ancient kingdoms, was organized around the myth of a universal community under a monarch who represented divinity. The God who liberated Israel from Egypt showed that every earthly kingdom and monarch exists by the grace of the one true God. Only God's kingdom is universal and omnicompetent. Moses was not a master monarch but a subordinate steward of the divine covenant. Moses was not an autocrat; he served under God's authority. Moses was not even omnicompetent within Israel; God's law made clear that priests and parents and other authorities each had distinguishable responsibilities before the Creator/Redeemer.[1]

The beginning of the Christian era further solidified this challenge to any earthly claim of omnipotence. Many early Christians refused to recognize the Roman Caesar as supreme lord because they recognized only Jesus Christ as Lord—as Israel's expected Messiah, as almighty God incarnate. Only the God revealed in Jesus Christ can be omnicompetent, they confessed. The mediator of God's new covenant did not claim a particular territorial kingdom on earth but reaffirmed divine authority over all kingdoms, over the whole earth. Moreover, in calling for repentance from sin and in offering redemption through his death and resurrection, Jesus Christ opened the way to the creation's eschatological fulfillment in the City of God. Christian faith has thus always challenged every utopian scheme to create a perfect kingdom on earth through purely human effort. Christian faith is entirely oriented by the confession that all things have been created by God, that human sinfulness distorts that good creation, and that only through Jesus Christ—God's ultimate Judge and Redeemer—will the creation (including human society) reach its fulfillment.

From this point of view, human beings—male and female—are, by creaturely constitution, related to God in all things. They are, through and through, the image of God. Human beings are utterly religious because all of life is related to God. Religion cannot be confined to church life even though there is a proper place for differentiated institutions of worship, communion, and pastoral oversight. God's relationship to his creatures shows up everywhere in creation. Moreover, this also means that every part of creation displays its own special value in God's scheme of things. So if God created people to develop as family members, scientific explorers, creative artists, caretakers of land and animals, educators, worshipers, and stewards of the public trust, then all of these differentiated talents and activities require the mutual respect of one another. The demand that justice be done to the structural diversity of the creation is built right into the creation.

But what if people do not recognize either the profound character of their religious nature or the created conditions for societal differentiation and integration? The inevitable result, from the biblical point of view, will be that humans will reach for something else to take the place of the omnipotent Creator-Redeemer in their lives. And when something in the creation is mistaken for God, then both it and every other part of the creation will be partially misunderstood, mislocated, and distorted in the process. Human disobedience against the will of God causes deep crises in the exercise of human responsibility.

False Images of the Polity

From a biblical point of view, not only should the Roman Caesar's claim to omnipotence have been denied, but other forms of political order also require reevaluation insofar as they display injustice. A human political order cannot itself be limitless, nor should it be confused with a particular community of faith. If membership in a civic community is based on church membership or on a particular profession of faith, then the political community cannot come into its own as a differentiated public-legal bond of citizenship among people of different faiths. From our point of view, therefore, it has been historically correct that caesaropapism and other kinds of church-state confusion should come to an end. Even in the United States, however, confusion remains with regard to the meaning of the separation of church and state. The existing confusion comes from two different civil-religious tendencies.

The Puritans helped engender one kind of confusion: their colony was an experiment in building a community that was neither a strictly qualified political order nor an exclusive society of faith within a wider political order. It was an ambiguous amalgam of the two. Church membership was a precondition for voting rights in the early Puritan colony, which to a degree remained tied to the English government. Due in large part to Puritan influence the entire American Republic eventually absorbed many characteristics of this ambiguous amalgam of religious community and political order: the United States became a nation with the soul of a church, as G. K. Chesterton once said.[2] Part of what makes it difficult even today for many Americans to think clearly about differentiating the political order from other spheres of society is that the "nation" remains the largest encompassing context of their lives. American nationalism still functions, in many respects, as the most common and most influential American religion—a civil religion.

But the Puritans are not solely responsible for this civil-religious confusion in American life. Jefferson and other civic republicans were seeking to build a different kind of "city on a hill." They did not use ancient Israel as their model but instead used the ideal of civic community inspired by Stoicism and Roman republicanism. Jefferson had no trouble with the idea of relegating dogmatic Christian "sects" to the sidelines. He wanted a different kind of faith community—a community of people who would develop their common moral sense and rationality in support of a government that would depend on the consensus of its citizens. Church membership could easily be dropped as a precondition for civic membership. But for Jefferson, a common moral ethos would have to be nurtured in the young through the common school (with a republican catechism) so that each would be able to function responsibly in the civic community. To this day, many Americans (perhaps the majority) see the nation—the American Republic—as the highest, broadest community of trust and moral allegiance to which they belong. As it did for many Roman republicans before them, this outlook has provided the integrating religion for many American lives. It inspires their deepest trust: America, the hope of the world, the greatest democracy on earth, the model of human community for the nations.[3]

From our point of view, neither of these forms of civil-religious nationalism expresses either right religion or a justly limited polity. Puritan and civic-republican compounds of state, nation, and religious community have encouraged resistance to the differentiation of multiple institutions and communities in American society.

Another distorting historical pattern that has been modified over time in American experience is the close connection of the political community to property ownership. We now affirm in law that all citizens, upon reaching maturity, have a right to vote and to participate politically whether or not they own property. But this was not always so. With roots reaching back into the feudal past, civic membership in early America was tied to the precondition of property ownership. Only a few white males met that condition. For good reasons, the separation of private property from political community has been accepted so that now we no longer tie the two together.

Nonetheless, a significant impetus from this older tradition continues to inspire religious passion and confusion among many. Some property owners who want to enjoy complete independence from government's intrusion into their personal fiefdoms consider the chief (if not sole) purpose of government to be the protection of their private property. Moreover, many Americans think of the United States chiefly as an economy whose government should serve as a means to the end of economic progress; they do not think of the United States first as a civic community. One of the reasons many citizens think about the polity in terms of a market or a business is because they think of America first of all as a land of economic opportunity in which anyone can own land and gain wealth through private enterprise. This was, in fact, the origin of some of America's earliest colonies. But political community, from our point of view, may not be reduced to economic opportunity, or to a means of protecting private property rights, or to a market in goods and services, or even to a community of economic justice.

Americans also continue to live with ambiguities about the relation of the political order to race, clan, family, and nation. Racism remains a serious problem in American society even though in most respects the legal/political order now defines civic membership and rights without regard to color, clan, or national identity. Healthy differentiation has taken place. The political community of "neighbors-in-law" is neither a family writ large, nor an extended clan, nor a race-based enclave. A state cannot be just and at the same time grant special privileges to a particular nation. If people of many races and nationalities live in the same civic order, each should be able to live equally as citizens under the law.

Where confusion about family, race, and nation most often arises today is in the use of analogical concepts drawn from family and clan life. The internal life of a family does happen to be highly undifferentiated. Children emerge into the larger, differentiated society by growing up within families in which parents play a number of roles in regard to their children—as nurturers, educators, worship leaders, friends, and more. When citizens and politicians think analogically of the United States as a "family" or talk about citizens as "brothers and sisters" who should care and serve one another, the analogy often leads to paternalistic and/or maternalistic expectations about government's services.

In 1760 Benjamin Stevens, a Congregational minister in Massachusetts, addressed the government officials of his day as "fathers of the people, whose duty it is to attend to the interest of the whole family."[4] In our day, Marian Wright Edelman, who recognizes that parents "bear the primary responsibility for meeting the needs of their own children,"[5] nonetheless makes liberal use of the family analogy when discussing the nation's responsibility for "its" children.

Without [citizens] losing sight of the broader vision of lifting every American child out of poverty and ensuring adequate health, child care, and educational opportunity for every child regardless of color or class, it is necessary to struggle constantly to define and package this vision in small, actionable bites. . . . Individuals and groups that care about the poor must fight constantly to translate laws and rights and policies into realities that improve the daily lives of children, families, the poor, elderly, and homeless. Like your own house, the national and community house gets dirty all the time unless someone cleans it up regularly.[6]

But the American Republic is no more a family or a household than it is a community of faith, or a feudal estate, or an economic market. The political community should not discriminate among citizens on the basis of their race, skin color, or family of origin. And for precisely that reason government should not displace families by means of government paternalism or maternalism.

Finally, in the minds of many, the political order is often thought of as an individual writ large. Whether conceived of as an autonomous, self-governing entity or as an organic unity of many parts, the "individual" becomes the metaphor for an independent, self-sufficient state. Another Massachusetts minister, Abraham Williams, preached a sermon in the early 1760s using the analogy this way:

As in the natural Body, the several Members have their distinct Offices, for which they are adapted, and when in their proper Order, they perform their natural Functions, the Body is in its most perfect State; so in the politic Body, when its several Orders attend to their respective Duties, proper to their Rank; the Welfare of the whole Community, and of every Individual, is secured and promoted.[7]

This, too, is an undifferentiated analogy or metaphor. If the United States is thought to be an autonomous, self-sufficient "body," then love of country may represent merely an extension or projection of self-love fueled by the autonomy ideal. The same individualistic citizens who want little or no government interfering in their lives at home may want a very strong military establishment to advance national autonomy in the international arena. The political order, under this inspiration, becomes an "individual rights" mechanism. The nation is not so much a complex civic *community* but a means to the end of individual self-realization and independence. On the world scene, the

United States is thus thought of not so much as one state among others, working cooperatively to secure international justice, but as an autonomous "individual" seeking to advance its own security and self-sufficiency.

Overcoming Mistaken Absolutizations

The purpose of this brief sketch is to hint at some of the reasons for conflict among American citizens who enter the political/legal arena with very different ideas of what a "healthy" America should look like. Different elements of society have, in each case, been absolutized and asked to answer the largest, deepest questions about life. The political order thus becomes a civil-religious whole for some people, or a universal market (or estate) for others, or an all-encompassing family or school for others, or the vanguard of individual autonomy for others. From the standpoint of each of these mistaken absolutizations, the other components of society are then reduced to mere cogs in the wheel, to mere means to other ends, to a subordinate function within the larger, undifferentiated "nation," "family," "faith community," "market," or "individual."

By contrast, we believe that even though the political/legal community properly embraces every citizen, the common civic bond should be of a specifically qualified type, serving the purpose of a public-legal integration that entails no right of omnicompetent authority and does not pretend to exhaust the communal nature of human society. The identity of a differentiated political order should be that of a civic-legal bond that unites citizens in the mutual and equitable sharing of the fruits and responsibilities of the commonwealth, which is made manifest through a constitutionally limited integration of every citizen and of every nongovernmental institution and community under laws of the Republic. Only by refusing to be an extended community of faith and by securing justice for all faith communities may a political community be religiously just. Only by refusing to be a family and by treating all families, races, and clans with equal justice can a political order perform its proper nurturing role. Only by resisting reduction to a market or an enterprising estate and by treating all enterprises, workers, and consumers equitably, can a political community uphold economic justice for all. Only by refusing to govern as the maximizer of individual autonomy and by protecting individual civic rights in the context of the fair treatment of all the institutions and associations of human society can a state properly foster individual freedom and cooperate with other states of the world in the pursuit of justice. In short, only by restricting itself to being a community of public-legal equity can the state do justice to all citizens and to the full panoply of moral responsibilities belonging to those citizens in their noncivic capacities.

No doubt there are other religious worldviews that can also make part of this case for a constitutionally limited, civic/legal integration of an open-ended, differentiated society. We welcome the prospects of testing our argument in dialogue with those who hold such views as well as with those who self-consciously wish to propound undifferentiated moral arguments in the political arena.

In any case, it should be clear that we wish to challenge citizens of all viewpoints to do two things. First, we believe that every citizen should engage in critical, self-conscious reflection on the deepest presuppositions about reality that control his or her approach to public life. Christians in particular, we believe, should not be so willing to accommodate themselves to civic-republican and other Enlightenment-influenced points of view. They should explore carefully the conflicts that have resulted from the apparent incompatibility of biblical and nonbiblical religions. They should seek to develop a coherent and comprehensive vision of God's creation order in which human society is differentiating historically and in which the political order ought to be understood as a limited public-legal community. This religious outlook is quite different from others which seek to eliminate God or to collapse all aspects of the complex creation order into an intramundane unity. Only to the extent that citizens truly engage one another at the level of their religious-root differences will it be possible to clarify the nature of their differences and thereby to discover the proper character of the civic bond that unites them as citizens.

Second, we challenge citizens to engage in debate about various public policies and legal matters by means of clearly differentiated moral discourse so that they can distinguish the particular responsibility of government from other institutional and associational responsibilities. If public moral discourse is not pursued in this way, we hypothesize that citizens will find themselves increasingly at odds in the public square in unnecessary ways, sinking into greater and greater confusion about what they expect any institution to be or to do. By means of differentiated moral discourse, which helps sort out distinguishable arenas of human responsibility, we believe it will be possible for citizens to gain a clearer idea of what a political community should be and of how it can do greater justice to all citizens in the rich diversity of their religious, cultural, and social obligations. Principled pluralism, both structural and confessional, can open the door to genuine civic community.

Introduction

1. Nathan Glazer and Daniel Patrick Moynihan, *Beyond the Melting Pot* (Cambridge, Mass.: M.I.T. Press, 1963); Michael Novak, *The Rise of the Unmeltable Ethnics* (New York: Macmillan, 1971, 1972).

2. George F. Will, *Restoration: Congress, Term Limits and the Recovery of Deliberative Democracy* (New York: Free Press, 1992). Will is a beneficiary of more than three decades of reinterpretation of the early American "republican" tradition by scholars such as Bernard Bailyn, Gordon Wood, and others. See, for example, Richard Beeman, Stephen Botein, and Edward C. Carter II, eds., *Beyond Confederation: Origins of the Constitution and American National Identity* (Chapel Hill: University of North Carolina Press, 1987).

3. Will, *Restoration*, p. 6.

4. W. Lance Bennett, *The Governing Crisis: Media, Money, and Marketing in American Elections* (New York: St. Martin's Press, 1992), p. 14. Books on the electoral and governing crises have been pouring off the presses in increasing numbers. See, for example, E. J. Dionne, Jr., *Why Americans Hate Politics* (New York: Simon and Schuster, 1991); William Greider, *Who Will Tell the People: The Betrayal of American Democracy* (New York: Simon and Schuster, 1992); Kevin Phillips, *Boiling Point: Republicans, Democrats, and the Decline of Middle-Class Prosperity* (New York: Random House, 1993); Donald L. Barlett and James B. Steele, *America: What Went Wrong?* (Kansas City: Andrews and McMeel, 1992); Herbert J. Gans, *Middle American Individualism: Political Participation and Liberal Democracy* (New York: Free Press, 1988); Ruy A. Teixeira, *The Disappearing American Voter* (Washington, D.C.: The Brookings Institution, 1992).

5. Arthur M. Schlesinger, Jr., *The Disuniting of America: Reflections on a Multicultural Society* (New York: W. W. Norton, 1991, 1992), p. 17. Literature on "multiculturalism" and various debates surrounding it is now extensive. Diverse examples include: Dinesh D'Souza, *Illiberal Education* (New York: Free Press, 1991); Ellen Carol DuBois and Vicki L. Ruiz, eds., *Unequal Sisters: A Multicultural Reader in U.S. Women's History* (New York: Routledge, 1990); Andrew Hacker, *Two Nations: Black and White, Separate, Hostile, Unequal* (New York: Scribner's, 1992); Charles Taylor, et al., *Multiculturalism and "The Politics of Recognition"* (Princeton: Princeton University Press, 1992); Benjamin R. Barber, *An Aristocracy of Everyone: The Politics of Education and the Future of America* (New York: Ballantine Books, 1992).

6. Shelby Steele, *The Content of Our Character* (New York: St. Martin's Press, 1990), p. 4. The arguments over race relations and racism in America continue to diversify. See, for example, Hacker, *Two Nations*; Stephen L. Carter, *Reflections of an Affirmative Action Baby* (New York: Basic Books, 1991); Douglas S. Massey and Nancy A. Denton, *American Apartheid: Segregation and the Making of the Underclass* (Cambridge: Harvard University Press, 1993); Carl T. Rowan, *Dream Makers, Dream Breakers: The World of Justice Thurgood Marshall* (Boston: Little, Brown, 1993); Toni Morrison, ed., *Race-ing Justice, En-gendering Power: Essays on Anita Hill, Clarence Thomas, and the Construction of Social Reality* (New York: Pantheon Books, 1992).

7. Robert N. Bellah, et al., *The Good Society* (New York: Knopf, 1991), p. 6. The communitarian critique of liberalism is now an established subdiscipline. See Robert N. Bellah, et al., *Habits of the Heart: Individualism and Commitment in American Life* (New York: Harper and Row, 1985); Philip Selznick, *The Moral Commonwealth: Social Theory and the Promise of Community* (Berkeley: University of California Press, 1992); Amitai Etzioni, *The Spirit of Community: Rights, Responsibilities, and the Communitarian Agenda* (New York: Crown Publishers, 1993); Alasdair MacIntyre, *After Virtue: A Study in Moral Theory*, 2d ed. (Notre Dame: University of Notre Dame Press, 1984); Michael J. Sandel, *Liberalism and the Limits of Justice* (Cambridge: Cambridge University Press, 1983); William Galston, *Liberal Purposes: Goods, Virtues, and Diversity in the Liberal State* (Cambridge: Cambridge University Press, 1991); Thomas A. Spragens, Jr., *The Irony of Liberal Reason* (Chicago: University of Chicago Press, 1981).

8. Mary Ann Glendon, *Rights Talk: The Impoverishment of Political Discourse* (New York: Free Press, 1991), p. 3.

9. Ibid.

10. Ibid.

11. Ibid., p. 14.

12. Ibid., p. 15. For more on the crisis of American law, see Glendon's *Abortion and Divorce in American Law* (Cambridge: Cambridge University Press, 1987); Harold J. Berman, *Law and Revolution: The Formation of the Western Legal Tradition* (Cambridge: Harvard University Press, 1983); Robert H. Bork, *The Tempting of America: The Political Seduction of the Law* (New York: Simon and Schuster Touchstone Books, 1990). Cf. also David Lyons, *Moral Aspects of Legal Theory* (Cambridge: Cambridge University Press, 1993).

13. Alan Wolfe, *Whose Keeper? Social Science and Moral Obligation* (Berkeley: University of California Press, 1989), p. 20.

14. Ibid., p. 5. In further critique of modernity, cf. Christopher Lasch, *The True and Only Heaven: Progress and Its Critics* (New York: W. W. Norton, 1991); and Leszek Kolakowski, *Modernity on Endless Trial* (Chicago: University of Chicago Press, 1990).

15. James Davison Hunter, *Culture Wars: The Struggle to Define America* (New York: Basic Books, 1991). Hunter is indebted to Peter Berger, as is his colleague Os Guinness who develops a similar evaluation of American society in *The American Hour* (New York: Free Press, 1993). See also Hunter and Guinness, eds., *Articles of Faith, Articles of Peace* (Washington, D.C.: The Brookings Institution, 1990); Peter L. Berger, *Facing Up to Modernity* (New York: Basic Books, 1977); Richard John Neuhaus, *The Naked Public Square* (Grand Rapids: Eerdmans, 1984).

16. Hunter, *Culture Wars*, p. 42.

17. Ibid., pp. 318, 325.

18. Ibid., p. 307.

19. Wolfe, *Whose Keeper?* p. 233.

20. Glendon, *Rights Talk*, pp. xiii, 183.

21. Bellah, et al., *Good Society*, pp. 283–86.

22. Steele, *Content*, p. 165.

23. Schlesinger, *Disuniting*, p. 18.

24. Bennett, *Governing Crisis*, p. 218.

25. Will, *Restoration*, pp. 179–83.

Chapter 1: *Foundations of Legal and Political Order*

1. It is not our intention here to enter into the intricate philosophical arguments among legal positivists, critical theorists, natural law thinkers, and others regarding the relation of law and government to morality. This first point, however, should not be taken to mean that we locate moral principles above or outside the arena that some imagine to be a merely technical legal realm. Rather, our assumption is closer to that which is expressed in the following statement by David Lyons: "[O]ne need not go beyond the law itself to find the basis for assessing it. One need not appeal to principles that have no necessary connexion with the law. But we are not required to say that unjust law somehow fails to exist. We may say instead that concepts of the law itself imply principles to be used in calling the law good or bad, just or unjust. When we understand what the law is then we see—not that all law is necessarily good and just—but *how to judge it*. The law thus carries within it principles for its own evaluation" (Lyons, *Moral Aspects of Legal Theory*, p. 2; and see further, pp. 64–101). With regard to morality and fundamental law in the constitution of a polity, compare ibid., pp. 141–201 with Bork, *Tempting of America*, pp. 139–85; with Eric Voegelin, "The Nature of the Law" (1957), in Voegelin's *The Nature of the Law and Related Writings*, ed. Robert Anthony Pascal, James Lee Babin, and John William Corrington (Baton Rouge: Louisiana State University Press, 1991, [vol. 27 of *The Collected Works of Eric Voegelin*]); and with David Novak, *Jewish Social Ethics* (New York: Oxford University Press, 1992), pp. 22–83. Cf. also Harold J. Berman, *Faith and Order: The Reconciliation of Law and Religion* (Atlanta: Scholars Press, 1993).

2. Steele, *Content of Our Character*, p. 17. Cf. Vaclav Havel, "Politics, Morality, and Civility," in idem, *Summer Meditations*, trans. Paul Wilson (New York: Knopf, 1992), pp. 1–20.

3. Schlesinger, *Disuniting of America*, p. 118.

4. Ibid., p. 35.

5. Glendon, *Rights Talk*, pp. 19–22.

6. Ibid., p. 23.

7. John H. Hallowell, *The Moral Foundation of Democracy* (Chicago: University of Chicago Press, 1954), passim.

8. Bellah, et al., *Good Society*, p. 265. The debate over liberalism is extensive. In addition to the works cited in note 7 of the Introduction, see Bruce A. Ackerman, *Social Justice in the Liberal State* (New Haven: Yale University Press, 1980); Ronald Dworkin, *Taking Rights Seriously* (Cambridge: Harvard University Press, 1977); idem, *Matter of Principle* (Cambridge: Harvard University Press, 1985); and John Rawls, *A Theory of Justice* (Cambridge: Belknap Press of Harvard University Press, 1971).

9. See, for example, Christopher Dawson, *Religion and the Rise of Western Culture* (New York: Doubleday Image Books, 1950); Berman, *Law and Revolution*; Herman Dooyeweerd, *Roots of Western Culture: Pagan, Secular, and Christian Options*, trans. J. Kraay, ed. Mark Vander Vennen and Bernard Zylstra (Toronto: Wedge Publishing Foundation, 1979); and R. H. Tawney, *Religion and the Rise of Capitalism* (New York: Mentor Books, 1926, 1954).

10. Hallowell, *Main Currents in Modern Political Thought*, p. 92. For more on the influence of the Enlightenment in early America, see Henry Steel Commager, *The Empire of Reason: How Europe Imagined and America Realized the Enlightenment* (Garden City: Doubleday Anchor Books, 1979); and Bernard Bailyn, *Ideological Origins of the American Revolution* (Cambridge: Harvard University Press, 1967).

11. Hallowell, *Main Currents*, p. 92. Cf. Wolfe, *Whose Keeper?* pp. 107–14.

12. See Roy Clouser, *The Myth of Religious Neutrality: An Essay on the Hidden Role of Religious Belief in Theories* (Notre Dame: University of Notre Dame Press, 1991).

Chapter 2: *Religions as Ways of Life*

1. Hunter, *Culture Wars*, p. 49.

2. Ibid., p. 57.

3. Ibid., p. 62. Cf. Clouser, *Myth of Religious Neutrality*, pp. 9–48.

4. Hunter, *Culture Wars*, p. 311.

5. With regard to the civil-religious aspect of this hypothesis, see the insightful argument of Wilbur Zelinsky, *Nation into State: The Shifting Symbolic Foundations of American Nationalism* (Chapel Hill: University of North Carolina Press, 1988). Referring to the work of Carlton Hayes, Zelinsky concludes that modern nationalism is a form of religion: "The rise of civil religion is another manifestation of modernization, and it has flourished in precise inverse relationship to the decay of conventional Christian dogma and practice or the erosion of other ancient faiths in an effort to fill the void left by their abdication from the hearts of humankind" (p. 233).

6. Schlesinger, *Disuniting*, p. 118.

7. Bellah, et al., *Good Society*, p. 182.

8. Ibid., p. 286.

9. Ibid., pp. 273–86. Phillip Hammond also uses slippery language in dealing with religion. In his insightful book, *The Protestant Presence in Twentieth-Century America* (Albany: State University of New York Press, 1992), Hammond writes that evangelicals today "are essentially correct on this one point at least: What they call 'secular humanism' *has* replaced Christian vocabulary as the major language of most of society's movers and shakers. In what other language *could* a rationale for a religiously diverse people be expressed?" (p. 17). Hammond's implication is that secular-humanist language alone is able to transcend religious diversity while remaining neutral among those religions. But that assumption is precisely what we are calling into question, and Hammond's own language exposes him. "In the face of expanding religious pluralism [in America]," says Hammond, "we uphold religious liberty as a value taking precedence over any of our particularistic creeds" (p. 18). While it may be true that those whose deepest "creed" (or most profound religious faith) is religious pluralism will see it as "taking precedence" over any other creed, Hammond's statement is certainly not true of those Americans who see religious freedom as grounded in Christian or Jewish norms of justice rather than in religious pluralism itself. A few sentences later, Hammond speaks of the "universal creed of religious liberty." His own argument, in other words, demands of him the use of religious language to articulate a creedal faith. His stance is not neutral above religions but is one religious confession among many. The very assumption that "religious liberty" is an expression of "secular humanism" rather than an expression of integral Christian faith is itself a deeply religious judgment. Hammond, no more than Schlesinger or Bellah and his colleagues, gives an account of his own religious language when discussing other religions from a standpoint that he presumes is not (but really is) religious.

10. Bellah, et al., *Good Society*, p. 181.

11. Ibid., p. 182. Our argument here is quite in sympathy with that of Rabbi David Novak who, in evaluating John Courtney Murray's attempt to construct a universalist public ethic, exposes the underlying religious-root differences in society that stymie Murray's attempt. "I have tried to show," writes Novak, "that the universal truth a Thomist like Murray assumed to be the correspondence with nature as a transcendent object cannot be constituted, for it requires a transcendence of traditions that is simply untenable for both philosophical and theological reasons. Surely, this does not mean, however, that transcendence cannot be affirmed and a correspondence theory of truth never employed. Both are indeed possible, but they are possible plurally, not singularly. Each tradition constitutes its *own* relationship with its *own* respective transcendent object. Judaism and Christianity each constitute their respective transcendent objects as the word of God. There are some areas of substantive overlap; there are more and deeper areas where there is none. In the case of the secular world, there is even much less overlapping with

Judaism or Christianity. But when there is overlapping between the secular and religious worlds, it is almost always at the point where the two religious traditions themselves overlap. Thus, there are only more specific truths and more general truths. Other than some basic logical truths, universal truth in theology or even philosophy will have to wait for the final redemption of the world. In the meantime, rationalities function within their respective traditions, a point Alasdair MacIntyre has helped us to understand better" (*Jewish Social Ethics*, pp. 79–80).

12. For more detailed development of the viewpoint underlying this argument, see James W. Skillen, "The Bible, Politics, and Democracy: What Does Biblical Obedience Entail for American Political Thought?" in *The Bible, Politics, and Democracy*, ed. Richard John Neuhaus, (Grand Rapids: Eerdmans, 1987); James W. Skillen, *The Scattered Voice: Christians at Odds in the Public Square* (Grand Rapids: Zondervan, 1990), esp. pp. 181–224; and James W. Skillen and Rockne M. McCarthy, eds., *Political Order and the Plural Structure of Society* (Atlanta: Scholars Press, 1991, [No. 2, Emory University Studies in Law and Religion, ed. John Witte, Jr.]), esp. pp. 1–27, 357–417.

Chapter 3: *The American Way of Life: An Endangered Species?*

1. Bellah, et al., *Good Society*, p. 181.
2. Hunter, *Culture Wars*, p. 42.
3. Ibid.
4. Ibid., pp. 44–45.
5. Bellah, et al., *Good Society*, p. 279.
6. For example, one would not know from reading Kevin Phillips' *Boiling Point* (which is about middle-class economic frustration) that there are any religious or constitutional questions in public dispute today. One would not suspect, after reading E. J. Dionne's *Why Americans Hate Politics* (which is about ideological polarization) that there is any problem in the legal system or in the structure of government. One would not learn from reading Andrew Hacker's *Two Nations* (which is about racism) that religious dispositions and differences have anything to do with the national crisis.
7. Wolfe, *Whose Keeper?* pp. 108–9.
8. Leszek Kolakowski explores this and other modern moral dilemmas in several fine essays. See especially "The Idolatry of Politics" in his *Modernity on Endless Trial*, pp. 146–61. Hedrick Smith, on the other hand, seems to suggest that there is no dilemma, but simply a need for Americans to enjoy the incongruity of untidiness side by side with neatness. After seven hundred pages, in which he details the messy and often disintegrating effects of the "power game" in Washington, Smith says, "[W]e now need political leadership that can provide not only vision but cohesion. . . . From a leader, from all of us, what is required is a tolerance of the untidiness of democracy, even genuine enjoyment in democracy's untidiness. . . . Our political system needs some neatening up. The power game will never be tidy. The competition will never quit. The ruckus will never quiet. But things will work better when people are encouraged to coalesce" (pp. 713–14).
9. Harold Berman speaks of the "West" whose legal foundations were laid in the eleventh and twelfth centuries this way: "'Israel,' 'Greece,' and 'Rome' became spiritual ancestors of the West not primarily by a process of survival or succession but primarily by a process of adoption: the West adopted them as ancestors. Moreover, it adopted them selectively—different parts at different times. Cotton Mather was no Hebrew. Erasmus was no Greek. The Roman lawyers of the University of Bologna were no Romans. . . . The West, from this perspective, is not Greece and Rome and Israel but the peoples of Western Europe *turning* to the Greek and Roman and Hebrew texts for inspiration, and *transforming* those texts in ways that would have astonished their authors. . . . The amazing thing is that such antagonistic elements could be brought together in a single world view" (*Law and Revolution*, p. 3).

10. Toward the end of the introduction to his *Law and Revolution*, Berman writes of the crisis in Western law (including American law) that it "is not merely a crisis in legal philosophy but also a crisis in law itself. Legal philosophers have always debated, and presumably always will debate, whether law is founded in reason and morality or whether it is only the will of the political ruler. It is not necessary to resolve that debate in order to conclude that as a matter of historical fact the legal systems of all the nations that are heirs to the Western legal tradition have been rooted in certain beliefs or postulates: that is, the legal systems themselves have presupposed the validity of those beliefs. Today those beliefs or postulates—such as the structural integrity of law, its ongoingness, its religious roots, its transcendent qualities—are rapidly disappearing, not only from the minds of philosophers, not only from the minds of lawmakers, judges, lawyers, law teachers, and other members of the legal profession, but from the consciousness of the vast majority of citizens, the people as a whole; and more than that, they are disappearing from the law itself" (p. 39).

11. Will, *Restoration*, p. 118.

12. Ibid., p. 119.

Chapter 4: *Recognizing the Differentiation of Society*

1. Glendon, *Rights Talk*, p. 67.

2. Ibid., p. 70.

3. Ibid.

4. Ibid., p. 48.

5. Ibid., p. 123. Glendon's quotation from Tribe is from the latter's *American Constitutional Law*, 2d ed. (Mineola, N.Y.: Foundation Press, 1988), p. 1416.

6. Wolfe, *Whose Keeper?* p. 10.

7. Glendon, *Rights Talk*, p. 120.

8. Wolfe, *Whose Keeper?* p. 2.

9. Bellah, et al., *Good Society*, p. 27.

10. Ibid.

11. See James W. Skillen, "Societal Pluralism: Blessing or Curse for the Public Good," in *The Ethical Dimension of Political Life*, ed. Francis Canavan (Durham, N.C.: Duke University Press, 1983), pp. 166–72; and idem, "Going Beyond Liberalism to Christian Social Philosophy," *Christian Scholar's Review*, vol. 19, no. 3 (March 1990): 220–30.

Chapter 5: *Public-Moral Argument in a Complex Social Order*

1. Wolfe, *Whose Keeper?* p. 120.

2. Ibid., p. 129.

3. Ibid., pp. 129–30.

4. Bellah, et al., *Good Society*, p. 143.

5. Ibid., p. 138.

6. Our concern here with the social complexity and differentiation is also of central concern to Michael Walzer in his *Spheres of Justice: A Defense of Pluralism and Equality* (New York: Basic Books, 1983) and to Jeffrey Stout in his *Ethics after Babel: The Languages of Morals and Their Discontents* (Boston: Beacon Press, 1988). See the critical discussion of these two in Skillen and McCarthy, eds., *Political Order and the Plural Structure of Society*, pp. 6–19.

7. Bellah, et al., *Good Society*, p. 146.

8. Ibid., p. 170.

9. Ibid., p. 175.

10. An excellent example of undifferentiated moral argument in regard to schooling is found in a recent statement by John R. Harrison, trustee of the Westminster Schools in Atlanta—an

independent Christian school that was put under pressure both by Harrison and by several leading universities used to admitting Westminster graduates. Harrison resigned from Westminster's board because he felt that the school should not be exclusive in hiring only Christian teachers. Harrison's statement when the board of trustees finally voted to end its policy of hiring exclusively Christian teachers was this: "I resigned to make the act of hiring discrimination very public and the immorality of it very clear" (*New York Times*, March 10, 1993). The "immorality," from our point of view, exists in the pressure to force a Christian school to back down from maintaining its own integrity. Harrison is using public-legal nondiscrimination criteria appropriate to civic discourse for what is not a governmental institution but a legitimately independent school.

11. Commenting on the national debate over homosexual exclusion from (or admittance to) the U.S. military, Robert P. Dugan, Jr., director of the public affairs office of the National Association of Evangelicals, writes: "Millions of Americans must be willing to say that homosexual activity is morally wrong, and to argue that our laws, military as well as civil, have their source in the moral law of God and the natural law foundational to our society and to all creation" (*NAE Washington Insight* [March 1993]). The moral judgment that homosexual practice is morally wrong is not sufficient to force the conclusion that military and civil law should keep gays out of the military—unless, of course, one is using an undifferentiated moral argument that does not allow for that distinction.

12. Bellah, et al., *Good Society*, p. 47.

13. Ibid., p. 260.

14. Ibid., p. 274.

15. Ibid., p. 275.

16. Hunter, *Culture Wars*, p. 177.

17. Ibid.

18. Ibid., pp. 312–13.

Chapter 6: *Structural and Confessional Pluralism*

1. Mary Ann Glendon and Raul F. Yanes, "Structural Free Exercise," *Michigan Law Review*, vol. 90 (December 1991): 544.

2. Ibid., p. 546.

3. Hunter, *Culture Wars*, p. 42.

4. Ibid., p. 43.

5. Ibid.

6. Ibid.

7. Ibid., pp. 35ff., 198ff.

8. Ibid., p. 201.

9. Both Kevin Phillips (*Boiling Point*) and E. J. Dionne, Jr. (*Why Americans Hate Politics*) also overlook or underestimate the influence of the political system's structure as they look for a new middle ground on which to overcome polarization in America. Dionne wants a new ideological center; Phillips expects to see a populist rise of "Middle Americans" who are out to regain their economic position. Whereas Hunter interprets polarization in moral terms, Dionne sees it in political-ideological terms and Phillips in economic terms. All three overlook the extent to which the political process forces citizens to fight for winner-take-all stakes, which in turn tends to force them into two opposing camps. Depending on the analyst's point of view (moral, ideological, economic), one can always find evidence of polarization because of these political dynamics.

10. Bennett, *Governing Crisis*, p. 163.

11. Will, *Restoration*, p. 108.

Chapter 7: *Individual and Institutional Rights*

1. This is also, in part, the argument of Stephen Carter's *Reflections of an Affirmative Action Baby*. Carter warns of the dangers of affirmative action while not rejecting it as strongly as Steele does. However, part of the reason for affirmative action and for other efforts to secure quotas of some kind is that African Americans and other minorities have no assurance of proportional representation in the legislative process. Straightforward majoritarianism in electoral politics always means that the majority's simplified "consensus" is imposed on everyone. The only way that some minorities can hope to "participate" equally is to fight for equal or proportionate *outcomes* of policies as a matter of minority right. Such an approach is backwards and *ex post facto*. It often results in the political or legal use of the principle of racial nondiscrimination to trump other criteria or qualifications that may be essential to the achievement of excellence in education, engineering, literature, science, or whatever. This is why proportionately just treatment of all citizens in family life, schooling, and political representation is essential if racial discrimination is to be overcome in public life.

2. Steele, *Content of Our Character*, p. 157.

3. Ibid., p. 173.

4. Ibid., pp. 159–60.

5. Ibid., p. 71.

6. William Pannell, in his *The Coming Race Wars? A Cry for Reconciliation* (Grand Rapids: Zondervan, 1993), makes the important argument from a Christian standpoint that overcoming racism requires reconciliation—something Christians are supposed to be especially equipped to pursue. Reconciliation at the religious-root level, as Pannell discusses it, will help overcome hatred and conflict in all institutions of society. But Pannell does not go further to elaborate the *political* implications of racial reconciliation. When he says that a "full-scale war of people groups" is brewing in the nation over the issue of power (p. 87), he raises the question, by implication, of how power ought to be justly distributed. But much of his book is a criticism of white misuse of power and of our racist culture rather than an articulation of how a just distribution of power can be achieved in a pluralistic, multicultural society. Reconciliation is, without doubt, essential in all social contexts, but even if different races stop hating one another, the question of the just distribution of political power remains to be answered.

7. Schlesinger, *Disuniting of America*, p. 137.

8. Ibid., p. 134.

9. Ibid., p. 137.

10. Carter, *Reflections of an Affirmative Action Baby*, pp. 243–54.

Chapter 8: *Exercising Religious Freedom*

1. See James W. Skillen, "Thomas Jefferson and the Religious Character of Education," *Religion and Public Education*, vol. 14, no. 4 (Fall 1987): 379–84; and David Little, "The Origins of Perplexity: Civil Religion and Moral Belief in the Thought of Thomas Jefferson," *American Civil Religion*, ed. in Russell E. Richey and Donald G. Jones (New York: Harper and Row, 1974), pp. 185–210.

2. Richard A. Baer, Jr., "The Supreme Court's Discriminatory Use of the Term 'Sectarian,'" *The Journal of Law and Politics*, vol. 6, no. 3 (Spring 1990): 449–68. The diversity of interpretations of the First Amendment today is actually greater than our basic contrast suggests. See the excellent assessment by Carl H. Esbeck, "A Typology of Church-State Relations in Current American Thought," in *Religion, Public Life, and the American Polity*, ed. Luis E. Lugo (Knoxville: University of Tennessee Press, forthcoming).

3. See, for example, Jefferson's letter of August 10, 1787, to his nephew Peter Carr in James B. Connant, *Thomas Jefferson and the Development of American Public Education* (Los Angeles: University of California Press, 1970), p. 102.

4. On American civil religion, see Zelinsky, *Nation into State*, esp. pp. 223–53; Sanford Levinson, *Constitutional Faith* (Princeton: Princeton University Press, 1988); Ruth H. Bloch, "Religion and Ideological Change in the American Revolution," in *Religion and American Politics: From the Colonial Period to the 1980s*, ed. Mark A. Noll (New York: Oxford University Press, 1990), pp. 44–61; Robert N. Bellah, *The Broken Covenant: American Civil Religion in Time of Trial* (New York: Seabury Press, 1975); Sidney E. Mead, *The Old Religion in the Brave New World: Reflections on the Relation between Christendom and the Republic* (Berkeley: University of California Press, 1977); and Hammond, *Protestant Presence in Twentieth-Century America*.

5. Michael McConnell, "Freedom from Religion," *The American Enterprise* (January/February 1993): 36. The literature on the religion clauses of the First Amendment is vast. See, for example, Mary Ann Glendon and Raul F. Yanes, "Structural Free Exercise," *Michigan Law Review*, vol. 90 (December 1991): 477–550; Hunter and Guinness, eds., *Articles of Faith, Articles of Peace*; William Lee Miller, *The First Liberty: Religion and the American Republic* (New York: Knopf, 1985); Richard E. Morgan, *The Supreme Court and Religion* (New York: Free Press, 1972); and A. James Reichley, *Religion in American Public Life* (Washington, D.C.: The Brookings Institution, 1985), pp. 115–67.

6. Sidney E. Mead, "The 'Nation with the Soul of a Church,'" in Richey and Jones, eds., *American Civil Religion*, pp. 70–71.

7. See Novak, *Jewish Social Ethics*, pp. 225–43; and Baer, "Supreme Court's Discriminatory Use of the Term 'Sectarian.'"

8. McConnell, "Freedom from Religion," p. 43.

9. Hunter, *Culture Wars*, p. 307.

Chapter 9: *Schooling in the Republic*

1. Bellah, et al., *Good Society*, p. 145.

2. Ibid., p. 146. See also Charles L. Glenn, Jr., *The Myth of the Common School* (Amherst: University of Massachusetts Press, 1988), pp. 63–178.

3. This is, for example, the presupposition of Benjamin Barber's *An Aristocracy of Everyone: The Politics of Education and the Future of America*. Much of the discussion that follows in the text is developed and documented more fully in McCarthy, Skillen, and Harper, *Disestablishment a Second Time*, pp. 15–51. See also James W. Skillen, ed., *The School-Choice Controversy: What Is Constitutional?* (Grand Rapids: Baker Books, 1993); idem, "Religion and Education Policy: Where Do We Go from Here?" *The Journal of Law and Politics*, vol. 6, no. 3 (Spring 1990): 503–29; and Rockne McCarthy, et al., *Society, State, and Schools: A Case for Structural and Confessional Pluralism* (Grand Rapids: Eerdmans, 1981).

4. Hunter, *Culture Wars*, p. 201.

5. See John E. Coons, "Intellectual Liberty and the Schools," *Journal of Law, Ethics and Public Policy*, vol. 1 (1985): 495–533.

6. Schlesinger, *Disuniting of America*, p. 75.

7. Ibid., p. 80.

8. Ibid.

9. Ibid., p. 90.

10. Ibid., p. 98.

11. Ibid.

12. Hunter, *Culture Wars*, pp. 197–224.

13. For an introduction to the arguments in favor of greater choice in schooling, see Clifford W. Cobb, *Responsive Schools, Renewed Communities* (San Francisco: ICS Press, 1992); Charles L. Glenn, Jr., *Choice of Schools in Six Nations* (Washington, D.C.: U.S. Department of Education, 1989); and Skillen, ed., *School-Choice Controversy*.

Chapter 10: *Public Discourse and Electoral Representation*

1. Bennett, *Governing Crisis*, p. 14.

2. Will, *Restoration*, p. 110.

3. Ibid., p. 117.

4. Ibid. Cf. William Greider, *Who Will Tell the People? The Betrayal of American Democracy* (New York: Simon and Schuster, 1992), pp. 35–59.

5. James L. Sundquist, *Constitutional Reform and Effective Government*, rev. ed. (Washington, D.C.: The Brookings Institution, 1992), pp. 178–79.

6. Will, *Restoration*, p. 92.

7. Ibid.

8. See Dionne, *Why Americans Hate Politics*, pp. 136–37. This criticism is not of recent vintage; see, for example, David Broder, *The Party's Over: The Failure of Politics in America* (New York: Harper and Row, 1971); and Martin P. Wattenberg, *The Decline of American Political Parties, 1952–1984* (Cambridge: Harvard University Press, 1986).

9. See Sundquist, *Constitutional Reform*, pp. 177–82; and Bennett, *Governing Crisis*, pp. 185–86.

10. Bennett, *Governing Crisis*, p. 163. Cf. Ruy A. Teixeira, *The Disappearing American Voter* (Washington, D.C.: The Brookings Institution, 1992), pp. 1–57; and Walter Dean Burnham, "The Turnout Problem," in *Elections American Style*, ed. A. James Reichley (Washington, D.C.: The Brookings Institution, 1987), pp. 97–133.

11. Bennett, *Governing Crisis*, p. 163. See also Martin P. Wattenberg, *The Rise of Candidate-Centered Politics* (Cambridge: Harvard University Press, 1991).

12. Will, *Restoration*, p. 19. Will's criticism here is related to problems associated with campaign financing and media manipulation that Bennett criticizes in detail (*Governing Crisis*, pp. 40–66). Cf. Larry Sabato, "Real and Imagined Corruption in Campaign Financing," in Reichley, ed., *Elections American Style*, pp. 155–79.

13. Bennett, *Governing Crisis*, pp. 5–6.

14. Ibid., p. 9. According to Bennett, "Instead of a principled national leadership with the power to govern by keeping the factions at bay, the leadership has been captured by the factions themselves. Therefore, instead of leading and governing, elected officials cannot do much beyond getting themselves reelected, and in order to do that, they must fashion the most delicate kind of political promises: the kind they cannot possibly hope to keep" (ibid., p. 64).

15. Ibid., p. 175. For a detailed argument explaining this form of declining government, see Theodore J. Lowi, *The End of Liberalism: The Second Republic of the United States* (New York: W. W. Norton, 1979).

16. Will, *Restoration*, pp. 9–10, 180ff.

17. Consider, for example, the following representative paragraph from Will's book: "It is possible, and I believe probable, that a reformed Congress would enjoy a reformed relationship with the electorate. A Congress purged of careerism would beget an electorate purged of its virulent cynicism about politicians, a cynicism born of suspicion about politicians' motives. From such a healthier relationship would come a greater willingness of citizens to trust government prudently to dispense the assets they have given up through taxation. This, in turn, would translate into a diminution of the taxaphobia that today is America's strongest—it sometimes seems to be the only strong—political passion" (ibid., p. 183).

18. For an introduction to proportional representation (PR) as it might affect American politics, see Michael Lind, "A Radical Plan to Change American Politics," *The Atlantic Monthly* (August 1992): 73–83; and Douglas Amy, *Real Choices/New Voices: The Case for Proportional Representation Elections in the United States* (New York: Columbia University Press, 1993). Cf. also Joseph F. Zimmerman, "The Federal Voting Rights Act and Alternative Election Systems," *William and Mary Law Review*, vol. 19, no. 4 (Summer 1978): 621–60. For more detailed his-

torical and comparative background, see Arend Lijphart and Bernard Grofman, eds., *Choosing an Electoral System: Issues and Alternatives* (New York: Praeger, 1984).

19. Changing from the American electoral system of single-member districts to a system of proportional representation for elections to the House of Representatives should not be confounded with the idea of changing from a presidential to a parliamentary system of government. The two do not have to go hand in hand. Lind ("Radical Plan") and Bennett (*Governing Crisis*, pp. 204–5) also support a change to PR for elections to the House, but Bennett does not develop the idea and Lind adds other details of complexity to the idea that seem to us unnecessary.

20. The change to PR for federal elections to the House of Representatives is even less complicated than implementing term limits. No constitutional amendment is necessary for a change to PR (see the U.S. Constitution, Art. I, Sec. 4). Lind, "Radical Plan," p. 76.

21. See Bennett, *Governing Crisis*, pp. 29–31.

22. The impossibility of achieving minority representation in a majority-rule electoral system is explained in John R. Low-Beer, "The Constitutional Imperative of Proportional Representation," *Yale Law Journal*, vol. 94, no. 1 (November 1984): 172–82. In the United States this question relates primarily to attempts to gerrymander single-member voting districts, often at court order, in order to achieve some kind of racial or other proportional representation in a state. In addition to Low-Beer's fine article, see also Sanford Levinson, "Gerrymandering and the Brooding Omnipresence of Proportional Representation: Why Won't It Go Away?" *UCLA Law Review*, vol. 33 (1985): 257–81; David R. Eichenthal, "Equal Protection III: Voting Rights, Political Gerrymandering, and Proportional Representation," *Annual Survey of American Law* (1987): 93–116; and Zimmerman, "Federal Voting Rights Act," pp. 626–40. Cf. Amy, *Real Choices/New Voices*, passim.

23. On the subject of thresholds, see Arend Lijphart and R. W. Gibberd, "Thresholds and Payoffs in List Systems of Proportional Representation," *European Journal of Political Research*, vol. 5 (1977): 219–44.

24. On this point, see Enid Lakeman, "The Case for Proportional Representation," in Lijphart and Grofman, eds., *Choosing an Electoral System*, pp. 46–7.

25. This is related to George Will's complaint about gerrymandering, but Will does not seem to realize that term limits will not even touch the problems associated with gerrymandering. See Will, *Restoration*, pp. 40–50.

26. On the German system, see Eckhard Jesse, "The West German Electoral System: The Case for Reform, 1949–87," *West European Politics*, vol. 10 (1987): 434–48; and Max Kaase, "Personalized Proportional Representation: The 'Model' of the West German Electoral System," in Lijphart and Grofman, eds., *Choosing an Electoral System*, pp. 155–64.

27. For the same reason of simplicity we will also forego consideration of another very responsible proposal, which is to augment representation by enlarging the House beyond its current limit of 435 seats. Michael Lind, for example, points out that if the United States today had the same proportion of population for each representative in the House as it did at the country's founding, there would now be eight thousand seats in the House ("Radical Plan," pp. 75–77). That is far too many, of course, but given the proportions in other countries, there is no reason why we should not have five hundred or six hundred or even more members in the House. Given the current crisis of confidence in government, however, the first reaction of many citizens to this idea would probably be fear—the fear that a larger number of House members would only add to the gridlock, corruption, and budget-busting tendencies of Congress. There is little point in considering such a change before evidence can be accumulated to show that strong national parties are able to exercise sufficient discipline and responsibility to make possible the enlargement of the House. Once it can be established that PR has helped restore government accountability, then a greater number of House seats would mean better rather than worse representation of the people.

28. Will, *Restoration*, pp. 180–81.

29. A change to PR represents a far more serious effort than does term limits to deal with the problem of an undeliberative Congress that has become subject to the passions of interest groups. Compare ibid., pp. 119–20; and Amy, *Real Choices/New Voices*, passim.

30. For background here, see Bennett, *Governing Crisis*, pp. 50–64.

31. See Richard S. Katz, "The Single Transferable Vote and Proportional Representation," in Lijphart and Grofman, eds., *Choosing an Electoral System*, p. 137.

Chapter 11: *In Defense of Justice for All*

1. For comparison of the biblical idea of the kingdom of God with the ancient Egyptian and Mesopotamian ideas of kingdom, see Eric Voegelin, *Israel and Revelation*, vol. 1 of *Order and History* (Baton Rouge: Louisiana State University Press, 1956); and John Bright, *The Kingdom of God* (Nashville: Abingdon Press, 1953). Cf. Novak, *Jewish Social Ethics*, pp. 1–66.

2. Quoted in Sidney E. Mead, "The 'Nation with the Soul of a Church,'" in Richey and Jones, eds., *American Civil Religion*, p. 45.

3. For readings on American civil religion, see note 4 of Chapter 8.

4. Quoted in Samuel Dunbar, *The Presence of God with His People, Their Only Safety and Happiness* (Boston: S. Kneeland, 1760), p. 64. For this quotation and the one acknowledged in note 7 below I wish to credit the doctoral dissertation of Dale S. Kuehne, "The Design of Heaven: Massachusetts Congregationalist Political Thought, 1760–1790" (Georgetown University, 1993).

5. Marian Wright Edelman, *Families in Peril: An Agenda for Social Change* (Cambridge: Harvard University Press, 1987), p. 33.

6. Ibid., p. 104.

7. Quoted in Charles S. Hyneman and Donald S. Lutz, eds., *American Political Writing During the Founding Era, 1760–1805* (Indianapolis: Liberty Press, 1983), p. 10.

Index